HELP!

MY JOB INTERVIEW IS TOMORROW!

How To Use The Library To Research An Employer

MARY ELLEN TEMPLETON

Neal-Schuman Publishers, Inc.

NEW YORK   LONDON

Published by Neal-Schuman Publishers, Inc.
100 Varick Street
New York, NY 10013

Printed and bound in the United States of America

Library of Congress Cataloging-in-Publication Data

Templeton, Mary Ellen.
    Help! My job interview is tomorrow! : how to use the library to
research an employer / Mary Ellen Templeton.
        p.   cm.
    Includes bibliographical references and index.
    ISBN 1-55570-089-6
    1. Vocational guidance--United States--Handbooks, manuals, etc.
    2. Business enterprises--United States--Information services.
    3. Reference books--Business--Bibliography.   4. Job hunting--United
States--Handbooks, manuals, etc.   I. Title.
    HF5381.T26   1991
    016.3387'0973--dc20   91-2680
                                                                                        CIP

For job seekers and
the librarians who help them

In memory of
Ellen Hitch Templeton,
mother and dedicated librarian

Contents

Acknowledgments

This book was written with the help of many friends and colleagues to whom I am very grateful. Edite Kroll, Martha McKay, Florence Blakely, Tanner Ottley Gay, Richard Levin, William Sharwell, Connie Dunlap, Robert Lesh, Tattie Roan, Mary Dawson, Judy Clarkson, Mary Lasher, Sally Dorst, Helen Patton, and Duane Parker contributed ideas and gave encouragement when the project was in its early stages.

My thanks go also to Betsey Patterson, George Fisk, George Parks, and Margaret Goggin who read the manuscript and offered valuable suggestions and to Andy Ambrose and Scott White who helped prepare the manuscript. Susan Holt of Neal-Schuman applied her editorial guidance with unfailing grace and good humor.

I am especially grateful to the library administration at Emory University for granting me a leave to begin the writing.

A Word to the Librarian

Requests for help in finding out about employers before job interviews occur frequently at library reference desks. My experiences as a graduate business student and as a business reference librarian have convinced me that while most job seekers know something about what an employer does, the most successful ones find out a good deal more. Armed with sound background information, they can ask the right questions that will ultimately lead to their own best job choices.

Books offering vocational guidance and advice about interviewing, including such classics as *What Color Is Your Parachute?* and *The Complete Job Search Handbook*, advise readers to do research on employers before going for interviews. They point out the usefulness of libraries in general and suggest book titles, but they can't give the kind of direct, specific guidance on the use of these sources that librarians are able to provide.

Guiding a person through the array of useful publications in this field is a time-consuming process. Librarians who are asked this question by users in a hurry or librarians at busy desks can seldom take the time to do more than show the inquirers a few places to get started.

Help! My Job Interview Is Tomorrow! makes it possible for a librarian to hand immediate help to anyone seeking information about an employer before an interview. It is organized to help users at several levels. People whose interviews are several hours away are likely to refer only to the worksheets to get answers to specific questions job seekers typically ask. Those with more time will want to read various chapters to get a better idea of some of the challenges and opportunities they may encounter in carrying out their research. While the book assumes users may be in a hurry, it also encourages them to plan ahead whenever possible for better results.

You will want to keep the book handy in your ready reference collection. Once a library's call numbers have been written on the worksheets or you have added any sources you might want to suggest in addition to the ones already there, the worksheets are ready to be used for quick access to works in your own reference collection. You may want to suggest to users that they photocopy worksheets they are likely to use repeatedly. Your library might make a supply of the worksheets available as handouts.

Help! My Job Interview Is Tomorrow! draws on publications commonly found in both academic and public libraries. A basic "how to," it is intended to be neither a formal bibliography nor a comprehensive business reference work. The bibliography at the end of the book will be useful as a checklist for collection development, and the index will serve as a detailed guide to the contents of the book.

Help! My Job Interview Is Tomorrow! is the guidance librarians would give if they had a few hours to spend with each job seeker. Hand it over as a lifesaver the next time someone says "Help!"

A Word to Job Seekers

Several years ago an otherwise outstanding business student rushed into a placement center and shouted: "Does anybody know anything about Corporation X? I have an interview with them in half an hour." Since no one within earshot could tell him anything useful about them, he went to the interview knowing only the name of the company. Not surprisingly, his first interview with that company was his last.

Accepting a position with an employer is something like entering into a marriage. A minimum of eight hours a day and a good deal of effort and psychic energy go into the bargain. You inherit an instant corporate "family," and history, and your personal fortunes are directly tied to the fortunes of the employer and the health of your working relationship.

Appearing for an interview without knowing anything much more about an employer than the organization's name and the time and place of the interview is like asking someone you just met to marry you. An interviewer can spot your ignorance at the outset and will wonder if you are really interested in the job or if you are there just for the money, the security or the prestige—in short, your own needs—since it will be apparent that you haven't made the effort to find out what their needs are.

In contrast, knowing as much as possible about an employer before the interview greatly improves the chances that you will establish yourself as a desirable candidate and in the end make the kind of well-informed choice that leads to a mutually rewarding partnership.

A job applicant need never be uninformed about an employer. Information on major U.S. corporations abounds. Information on smaller or privately held companies and not-for-profits of various kinds can be more difficult to locate, but using this book, you should be able to work to find whatever useful information is available in a library.

Help! My Job Interview is Tomorrow! is not intended to be read from cover to cover. Find the chapter you need, and if you have time, read the text. If you are in a hurry, go straight to the worksheets at the end of the chapter.

You may want to make a photocopy of the worksheets you use for future reference if you are going to be interviewing with a number of similar employers. Punch holes in the worksheets and keep them in a notebook. Then if you photocopy pages from sources or take notes on the employers you research and keep them behind the worksheets, you'll have an easy way to keep track of what you found and where you found it.

Tomorrow's interview could lead to a great match.

1
How to Prepare for an Interview Today

About Resources

The mystique surrounding business information can make us assume mistakenly that most of the useful information about a company is available only to insiders. While it is true that much useful information about a company can come from the inside, outsiders such as the company's clients, customers, suppliers, affiliates, or employment counselors, professors, consultants, and others who know the company, as well as libraries, can be rich sources of information about employers.

Of course, if you have access to information from the inside through any kind of a network—friends, relatives, alumni or placement offices, you should take full advantage of this opportunity to get valuable first-hand information.

For students, school placement officers usually keep files of materials furnished by recruiting companies: annual reports, brochures, reprints of stories from newspapers and magazines, etc. Placement officers may be able to refer students to recent graduates working for employers of interest, or to faculty members who may have first-hand information from their consulting or other work in the field.

Some placement offices maintain libraries with books on careers, types of jobs available in various fields, and directories listing businesses or organizations such as government or other not-for-profit employers. These are particularly useful if your best potential employer doesn't recruit at your school.

If you are looking for a first job or are changing jobs, similar resources are often available in college and university libraries, some public libraries, and bookstores. They may also be found in the offices of commercial

1

placement services. Job changers may have an easier time getting information especially if they have already established personal contacts in their fields, or have access to special libraries or the services of executive recruiters or other commercial placement services.

As you are deciding which resources to use for your research, remember that libraries vary greatly in their usefulness: small public libraries and branches will be likely to have information useful to individual investors and small businesses; large public libraries will tend to serve those groups and larger businesses as well. Academic business collections usually support the teaching, research, and consulting carried on in the schools where they are. Special libraries maintain whatever specialized materials the group supporting them needs.

If you are not a regular member of the constituency of one of these types of libraries, you may not necessarily be given access or service there. You need to check that out beforehand. If you are working in a specialized field like hotel management or the retail grocery business, you may also need to call ahead to be sure they have the materials you need before you make a trip. Most libraries will suggest other collections if theirs aren't suited to your needs.

It's a good idea to get acquainted with the library you plan to use before you need to use it. You'll learn about its hours of operation, what kind of business collection and working facilities it has, and what limitations there might be on your use of it. For example, many of the sources listed here are known as "reference" sources and can't be removed from most libraries. You won't be able to borrow them, but you'll also be sure they'll be in the library when you need them. *Help! My Job Interview is Tomorrow!* will help you find much of the information you'll need without stopping to ask anyone for help in the library. With this book or some of the worksheets in hand, you can go directly to the sources you need to answer your questions. If you do get stuck or have trouble finding one of the titles mentioned, or need additional help, ask a reference librarian for help.

One word of caution: reference librarians are often asked to help people who have job interviews in a few hours find information about the company. Some of the problems the librarians encounter in that situation will be your problems too. If there are a lot of people waiting to ask questions, the reference librarian won't be able to give you much time or extended help. If the company is small, neither one of you may be able to find much information about it in the library in a short time—or even a long time. Maybe an online, computerized search is just what it would take to find the kind of business information you need, but most reference departments don't perform these searches on the spur of the moment.

If you come to the library with more than a few hours to do your work, and the reference librarians aren't trying to help a crowd of people, you can talk with one of them at some length about your research project. The librarian may be able to suggest more useful sources to you—both in your library and elsewhere. If you find your library can't supply your needs, ask the reference librarian to suggest other places to look for information. Chapters 4, 5, and 6 will help you, but your librarian may know special sources of information available locally such as special libraries, clipping files, and information brokers. Your results will be better, and you'll both be happy.

What Do You Want To Find Out?

You have an appointment for an interview. You already know a little about the company. Before they offer you a job, the company will want to know two important things about you: how much you're likely to contribute to the company, and how well you'll "fit" there.

While they will make an effort to interest you in the position, if you are in competition with others, you'll have to sell yourself to win the job. The selling will begin as soon as they start to learn about you. They already may have asked for your resume to find out about your training, experience, interests, etc.

In the course of the interview, they will probably ask you why you are interested in this job and why you want to work for their company in particular. If you know about the company's present and past, its goals and challenges, you can answer the interviewer's questions in ways that will show how you meet the unique needs of the job and the organization. Without showing off what you know, you can use the information you've found to sell yourself.

If you are well informed about the company, the interviewer will know you cared enough to learn about it—that for you, not just any company will do. You will have done your part to demonstrate part of the "fit" between you and the organization. If you are competing with other equally employable but less informed candidates, you'll have an advantage.

Once you're past the first interview, you will probably want to know more about what the company has to offer you so that you can decide if their job really is your own best opportunity. If you have a few minutes now, you might find it helpful to make your own list of things you'd want to know about a company before going for an interview. Make a second list of things you'd expect to find out later before accepting employment.

You might compare your lists with these suggested by graduate business students in the years I've been asking them to make the same lists.

Before the Interview
- address, telephone number of company headquarters
- other locations, branches, divisions
- nature of the business

- products, services, etc.
- names of corporate officers
- size of staff
- stock exchange
- financial information: sales, profitability, efficiency, etc.
- competitive strength, rank of company in industry
- biographical information about the officers
- history of the company
- potentially critical problems
- new developments: products, services, facilities, methods, mergers, acquisitions, etc.

Before Accepting the Job

- personal fit
- corporate culture
- affirmative action programs
- opportunities for advancement
- staff turnover
- attitude of employees toward the company
- morale
- corporate climate
- educational opportunities
- training programs
- support for career progress
- organizational chart
- communications within the organization
- career paths for specific hiring situations
- compensation for the position under discussion

Some of the most important questions you should ask in the overall process of interviewing may not be answerable by consulting sources in the library. These questions usually must be answered by personal sources, publications issued by the employer in question, or a visit to the job site. If your interview really is tomorrow, you will probably be able to get help with only very few of these questions, if any at all, before the interview. For example, questions about topics like these usually require a conversation with someone well acquainted with work in the organization. This person could be a friend, an alumnus of your school, a relative, or someone else with whom you can speak personally and in confidence:

- personal fit
- corporate culture
- affirmative action programs
- opportunities for minorities
- staff turnover
- attitude of employees toward company

- morale in the office, department, division, company as a whole
- corporate climate

Specific techniques for acquiring job-related information from other people and your own personal observations, rather than library resources, are outside the scope of this book. Excellent guidance in that area can be found in:

What Color is Your Parachute? by Richard Nelson Bolles
Sweaty Palms; the Neglected Art of Being Interviewed by H. Anthony Medley
The Complete Job Search Handbook by Howard Figler

Literature the company supplies to applicants or placement offices sometimes will answer questions in these areas:

- promotion from within
- benefits
- opportunities to further education
- support for career progress

Other questions are often answered in interviews:

- communications within the organization?
- organizational chart?
- career paths for specific hiring situations?

One question is usually answered definitively toward the end of the interviewing process: compensation for the specific position under discussion.

Some of the questions above can also be answered by your own observations when you visit the site—usually after your initial interview. Articles and books you will find in the library can help with some of these questions, but the answers usually appear by chance. Reading as many recent articles as possible can be helpful if you have the time, but getting an answer to any of these questions in particular will largely be a matter of luck.

This is true of possibly the most important question of all—your personal fit with the organization. Why is this so important? In his book, *Power and Influence*, Professor John Kotter of the Harvard Business School says that if you are not in sync with the rest of the people you work with, you are destined to be able to accomplish very little in your job.

Kotter observes that many people take jobs early in their careers because they pay well or appear somehow glamorous or attractive rather than considering how well they are likely to fit in the organization. Getting things done, especially if you supervise others, depends greatly on your ability to gain the respect and support of people in the organization—above, beside, and below you.

Finding factual answers to important questions can give you some basis for your decision about whether or not you and the employer are a match, but your individual judgment will be equally important in reaching your optimal choice. The best strategy for any person discussing a position with an employer is to use a combination of objective and intuitive information. This book helps with objective information; the intuitive aspect will be largely up to you.

2
If Your Interview Is This Afternoon

Quick and dirty is the best description of most people's research in this situation. If you are interviewing with a corporation, you're in some luck. Go immediately to the business reference collection, take this book along, and work efficiently. You should be able to uncover a reasonable quantity of information about any major employer in two hour's time.

If you are dealing with a small, very new, or closely held company, you are going to have a harder, maybe impossible, time finding information quickly. Turn to Chapter 4 and Chapter 5 for help.

If you are researching a large, publicly held corporation, the reference librarian can usually point out many common sources if you'll present the list of titles on the worksheet which follows. The books are probably near each other on the shelves. If you have to look up all the titles in the library's catalog, you'll delay starting your research.

The First Fifteen Minutes: Your best bet is to begin with one of the directories cited in Section I of the worksheet. There, in just a few minutes, you can find out the exact name of the company, its address, telephone number, names of its officers, its recent revenues, number of employees, where its stock is traded, the names of the members of the board, and the company's products.

The Next Half Hour: You can get some comparative information about the company by using the sources in Section II of the worksheet. There you will find how it ranks among other large corporations and among other companies in its field. In the process of doing this, you'll get some idea of the company's relative financial strengths and weaknesses.

The Next Fifteen Minutes: If the company is very large, you may find one or more of its officers listed in the directories in Section III. Biographical sketches of these people may suggest what the company as a whole values in its employees.

The Rest of the Time You Have Left: To learn more of the past, present, and probable future of the company, go to any of the first three sources cited in Section IV. If you find you still have time, read periodical and newspaper articles you find by using the indexes already listed on the worksheet. Look for the name of the company in the indexes.

Don't expect to get to Section V unless you find some extra time! It's there in case you do.

Good luck!

-WORKSHEET-

INFORMATION	WHERE TO FIND IT

-I-

Call no.

name, address, telephone no. of company headquarters; names of officers; size of corporate staff; sales, products, services	_____ Standard & Poor's Register of Corporations, Directors, and Executives
	_____ Dun & Bradstreet Million Dollar Directory
	_____ Thomas Register of American Manufacturers
divisions, subsidiaries, affiliates	_____ Directory of Corporate Affiliations
	_____ America's Corporate Families: The Billion Dollar Directory

-II-

rank of company among large corporations (with assets, net income, sales, no. employees)	_____ Fortune Directory
	_____ Forbes, "Annual Directory Issue," each April
rank of company among large corporations (with stock-holders' equity, earnings per share, growth in earnings per share)	_____ Fortune Directory
	_____ Forbes, "Annual Report on American industry," each January
standing of a company in its industry or field	_____ Value Line Investment Survey
	_____ Standard & Poor's Industry Surveys

<table>
</table>

INFORMATION	WHERE TO FIND IT
	_____ <u>Forbes</u>, "Annual Report on American Industry," each January
	_____ <u>Business Week</u>, "Corporate Scoreboard," each March
	_____ <u>Fortune Directory</u> including rankings of the largest diversified service companies, commercial banking cos., life insurance cos., retailing cos., diversified financial cos., transportation cos., utilities

-III-

biographical information about the officers	_____ <u>Who's Who in Finance and Industry</u>
	_____ <u>Standard & Poor's Register of Corporations, Directors, and Executives</u>
	_____ <u>Reference Book of Corporate Managements</u>
	_____ <u>Who's Who in America</u>
	_____ <u>Business Index</u>
	_____ <u>Business Periodicals Index</u>
	_____ <u>Wall Street Journal Index</u>
	_____ <u>New York Times Index</u>

INFORMATION	WHERE TO FIND IT
	_____ National Newspaper Index
	-IV-
history of the company	_____ Moody's Manuals (also give historical financial data)
	_____ Standard & Poor's Corporation. Standard Corporation Descriptions.
	_____ annual reports, 10-K reports
	_____ company published brochures
	_____ books (See library catalog under name of company)
	_____ journal articles. See Business Index; Business Periodicals Index; Predicasts F&S Index United States under the name of company
	_____ newspaper articles. See New York Times, Wall Street Journal, or National Newspaper indexes
	-V-
potentially critical problems	_____ annual reports, 10-K reports
	_____ Moody's Manuals
	_____ Standard & Poor's Corporation. Standard Corporation Descriptions.

<u>INFORMATION</u>   <u>WHERE TO FIND IT</u>

                                  _____ periodicals and newspapers

plans for new products, facilities,   _____ annual reports, 10-K
services, methods, mergers,   reports
acquisitions, etc.
                                  _____ <u>Value Line Investment Survey</u>

                                  _____ journal and newspaper
                                               articles (See journal and
                                               newspaper indexes cited
                                               above.)

3
If Your Interview Is in a Few Days

If your job interview is not this afternoon, but a few days away, you are in a position to prepare well. With several or more hours in the library, you'll have time to find most of the information you need. You'll also have time to think of ways to use it effectively in your interview.

Take a few minutes to look over this chapter, and you'll have a good idea of what you can expect to find once you start your work in the library. To get an idea of the kind of information you can expect from each of the sources on the worksheet for this chapter, we'll take a few minutes to look through each of them to see how they present one large company, International Business Machines Corporation. If you are working on a large corporation of any kind: a bank, insurance company, an airline, retailer, etc., and if it's publicly owned, you should find similar information in these sources. If you are dealing with a small business, or a larger privately owned one, you need to refer to Chapter 4 or Chapter 5.

Directories

The first five titles on the worksheet make up a group of directories. We usually think of directories as sources of names, addresses, and telephone numbers. All of these supply that information, but they do more. Let's take a look at *Standard & Poor's Register of Corporations, Directors, and Executives,* Volume 1 and see what it tells us about IBM (Figure 3-1):

We have the name of the company.
We have its address (corporate headquarters).
We have its telephone number.
We have the names of the officers.

FIGURE 3-1. Sample entry from *Standard and Poor's Register of Corporations and Executives.*

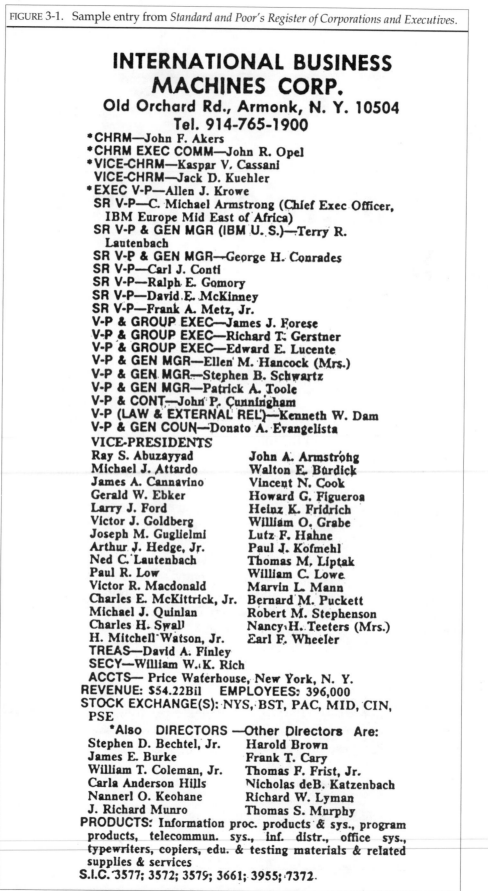

INTERNATIONAL BUSINESS MACHINES CORP.
Old Orchard Rd., Armonk, N. Y. 10504
Tel. 914-765-1900
* CHRM—John F. Akers
* CHRM EXEC COMM—John R. Opel
* VICE-CHRM—Kaspar V. Cassani
  VICE-CHRM—Jack D. Kuehler
* EXEC V-P—Allen J. Krowe
  SR V-P—C. Michael Armstrong (Chief Exec Officer, IBM Europe Mid East of Africa)
  SR V-P & GEN MGR (IBM U. S.)—Terry R. Lautenbach
  SR V-P & GEN MGR—George H. Conrades
  SR V-P—Carl J. Conti
  SR V-P—Ralph E. Gomory
  SR V-P—David E. McKinney
  SR V-P—Frank A. Metz, Jr.
  V-P & GROUP EXEC—James J. Forese
  V-P & GROUP EXEC—Richard T. Gerstner
  V-P & GROUP EXEC—Edward E. Lucente
  V-P & GEN MGR—Ellen M. Hancock (Mrs.)
  V-P & GEN MGR—Stephen B. Schwartz
  V-P & GEN MGR—Patrick A. Toole
  V-P & CONT—John P. Cunningham
  V-P (LAW & EXTERNAL REL)—Kenneth W. Dam
  V-P & GEN COUN—Donato A. Evangelista
  VICE-PRESIDENTS

Ray S. Abuzayyad	John A. Armstrong
Michael J. Attardo	Walton E. Burdick
James A. Cannavino	Vincent N. Cook
Gerald W. Ebker	Howard G. Figueroa
Larry J. Ford	Heinz K. Fridrich
Victor J. Goldberg	William O. Grabe
Joseph M. Guglielmi	Lutz F. Hahne
Arthur J. Hedge, Jr.	Paul J. Kofmehl
Ned C. Lautenbach	Thomas M. Liptak
Paul R. Low	William C. Lowe
Victor R. Macdonald	Marvin L. Mann
Charles E. McKittrick, Jr.	Bernard M. Puckett
Michael J. Quinlan	Robert M. Stephenson
Charles H. Swall	Nancy H. Teeters (Mrs.)
H. Mitchell Watson, Jr.	Earl F. Wheeler

  TREAS—David A. Finley
  SECY—William W. K. Rich
  ACCTS— Price Waterhouse, New York, N. Y.
REVENUE: $54.22Bil   EMPLOYEES: 396,000
STOCK EXCHANGE(S): NYS, BST, PAC, MID, CIN, PSE
     * Also DIRECTORS —Other Directors Are:

Stephen D. Bechtel, Jr.	Harold Brown
James E. Burke	Frank T. Cary
William T. Coleman, Jr.	Thomas F. Frist, Jr.
Carla Anderson Hills	Nicholas deB. Katzenbach
Nannerl O. Keohane	Richard W. Lyman
J. Richard Munro	Thomas S. Murphy

PRODUCTS: Information proc. products & sys., program products, telecommun. sys., inf. distr., office sys., typewriters, copiers, edu. & testing materials & related supplies & services
S.I.C. 3577; 3572; 3579; 3661; 3955; 7372.

FIGURE 3-2. Sample entry from the *Directory of Corporate Affiliations*.

I(INTERNATIONAL)

Section 2 — Parent Companies

INTERNATIONAL BROADCASTING
CORPORATION—(Continued)

Lakewood, CO 80215
Tel.: 303-298-5300

Subsidiaries:

8296-062

Century Park Pictures (1)
1901 Ave. of The Stars
Los Angeles, CA 90067
Tel.: 213-203-9933   (55.8%)
Motion Picture Film Production
S.I.C.: 7384
Phil Rogers (Pres.)

Subsidiary:

8296-063

Bietak Productions (2)
12315 Palms Blvd.
Los Angeles, CA 90066
Tel.: 213-390-8589   (50.1%)
Develops, Produces & Operates Small Ice
Shows
S.I.C.: 7922
Willie Bietak (Pres.)

8296-008

Harlem Globetrotters, Inc. (1)
6121 Santa Monica Blvd.
Hollywood, CA 90038
Tel.: 213-469-2767
S.I.C.: 7941
Joseph Zivino (Gen. Mgr.)

8296-009

Ice Capades, Inc. (1)
6121 Santa Monica Blvd.
Hollywood, CA 90038
Tel.: 213-469-2767
S.I.C.: 7922
David Hauser (Show Opers.)
Frank Hamilton (Mktg.)

Division:

8296-064

Ice Capades Chalets Division (2)
6121 Santa Monica Blvd.
Hollywood, CA 90038
Tel.: 213-469-2767
Recreational Ice Skating Facilities
S.I.C.: 7999
Michael Booker (V.P.)

† *   7871-000

INTERNATIONAL BUSINESS
MACHINES CORPORATION
Old Orchard Rd.
Armonk, NY 10504
Tel.: 914-765-1900   NY
IBM—(NYSE PS Bo Ci MW Ph Ts
BRU DUS GEN LON PARIS
TOKYO VIEN)
Assets: $73,037,000,000
Earnings: $5,806,000,000
Liabilities: $33,528,000,000
Net Worth: $39,509,000,000
Approx. Sls.: $59,681,000,000
Emp: 387,112
Fiscal Year-end: 12/31/88
IBM Information Handling Systems;
Data Processing Machines and
Systems; Program Prods.,
Telecommunications Systems, Office
Systems, Typewriters, Copiers,
Educational & Testing Materials &
Related Supplies &Services
S.I.C.: 3571; 3572; 3575; 3577; 3579;
3695; 3861; 3955; 7371; 7372; 7373;
7374; 7375; 7376; 7377; 7378; 7379;
3661; 3669; 8748
John F. Akers (Chm. Bd. & Chief Exec.
Officer)
Jack D. Kuehler (Pres.)
C. Michael Armstrong (Sr. V.P. & Chm.
& Pres.-IBM World Trade Corp.)
Walton E. Burdick (Sr. V.P.-Personnel)
George H. Conrades (Sr. V.P. & G.M.-
US Mktg. & Services)
Terry R. Lautenbach (Sr. V.P. & G.M.-
IBM United States)
David E. McKinney (Sr. V.P.-IBM World
Trade Europe/Middle East/Africa)
Frank A. Metz, Jr. (Sr. V.P.-Fin. &
Plng.)
Ray S. AbuZayyad (V.P. & Pres.-ROLM
Systems Corp.)
John A. Armstrong (V.P.-Science &
Technology)
Michael J. Attardo (V.P. & Pres.-Gen.
Technology Div.)

Carl J. Conti, Sr. (V.P. & G.M.-
Enterprise Systems)
Patrick A. Toole (Sr. V.P. & G.M.-
Technology Prods.)
Kenneth W. Dam (V.P.-Law & External
Rels.)
Gerald W. Ebker (V.P. & Pres.-Systems
Integration Div.)
Donato A. Evangelista (V.P. & Gen.
Counsel)
Larry J. Ford (V.P.-Information &
Telecommunications)
James J. Forese (V.P. & Grp. Exec.-
IBM World Trade Americas)
Heinz K. Fridrich (V.P.-Mfg.)
Richard T. Gerstner (V.P. & G.M.-
Personal Systems)
Victor J. Goldberg (V.P.-Mgmnt
Systems & Organization-IBM U.S.)
William O. Grabe (V.P. & Asst. G.M.-US
Mktg. & Services)
Joseph M. Guglielmi (V.P. & Pres.-
Application Systems Div.)
Ellen M. Hancock (V.P. & G.M.-
Communication Systems)
Arthur J. Hedge, Jr. (V.P.-Real Estate &
Construction)
Hans-Olaf Henkel (V.P. & Pres.-IBM
Germany)
Robert J. LaBant (V.P. & G.M.-Market
Opers.)
Ned C. Lautenbach (V.P. & G.M.-
Application Solutions)
Paul R. Low (V.P. & Pres.-General
Prods. Div.)
Edward E. Lucente (V.P. & Grp. Exec.-
IBM World Trade Asia/Pacific Grp.)
Marvin L. Mann (V.P. & G.M.-Service
Industries)
David E. McDowell (V.P. & Pres.-Natl.
Service Div.)
Charles E. McKittrick, Jr. (V.P.-
Governmental Programs)
Ennio Presutti (V.P. & Pres.-IBM Italy)
M. Bernard Puckett (V.P.-Data Systems
Div.)
Peter M. Schneider (V.P.-Systems &
Programming)
Stephen B. Schwartz (V.P. & G.M.-
Application Business Systems)
Takeo Shiina (V.P. & Pres. & Chief
Exec. Officer-IBM Japan)
Robert M. Stephenson (V.P. & Asst.
G.M.-IBM United States)
Nancy H. Teeters (V.P. & Chief
Economist)
John M. Thompson (V.P. & Pres. &
Chm.-IBM Canada)
H. Mitchell Watson, Jr. (V.P. & Pres. &
Chief Exec. Officer-Rolm)
Earl F. Wheeler (V.P. & G.M.-
Programming Systems)
John P. Cunningham (V.P. & Controller)
James A. Cannavino (V.P. & Pres.-
Entry Systems Div.)
Robert J. Corrigan (V.P. & Pres.-
Systems Technology Div.)
James Dezell (V.P. & G.M.-IBM
Educational Systems)
Nicholas M. Donofrio (V.P. & Pres.-
Advanced Workstations Div.)
Howard G. Figueroa (V.P.-Comml. &
Indus. Rels.)
Lucie J. Fjeldstad (V.P. & G.M.-
Academic, General & Public Sector
Indus.)
Harry Kavetas (V.P.& Pres.-IBM Credit
Corp.)
Edward J. Kfoury (V.P. & G.M.-
Industrial Sector)
William W. K. Rich (Sec.)
Robert M. Ripp (Treas.)
Board of Directors:
John F. Akers
Stephen D. Bechtel, Jr.
Harold Brown
James E. Burke
Frank T. Cary
William T. Coleman, Jr.
Thomas F. Frist, Jr.
Nicholas deB. Katzenbach
Nannerl O. Keohane
Jack D. Kuehler
Richard W. Lyman
J. Richard Munro

Thomas S. Murphy
John R. Opel
Helmut Sihler
John B. Slaughter
Edgar S. Woolard, Jr.
                          28223-000
First Chicago Trust Company of New
York(Transfer Agent)
30 W. Broadway
New York, NY 10007-2192
Tel.: 212-587-6515
                          22610-000
Wells Fargo Bank(Transfer Agent)
420 Montgomery St.
San Francisco, CA 94104
Tel.: 415-396-0123

Information Systems & Storage
Group:

Operating Units:
                          7871-134
IBM Application Business Systems (1)
472 Wheelers Farms Rd.
Milford, CT 06460
Tel.: 203-783-7000
Develops & Mfgs. Midrange Processors &
Related Software, Operating Systems&
Storage Devices
S.I.C.: 3571; 3572; 7372
Stephen B. Schwartz (V.P. & Gen. Mgr.)
                          7871-135
IBM Application Solutions (1)
1133 Westchester Ave.
White Plains, NY 10604
Tel.: 914-642-3000
Develops Solutions for IBM Customer
Application Problems; Application
Development, Systems Integration,
Professional Srvcs. & Market Development
S.I.C.: 7373; 7379
Ned C. Lautenbach (V.P. & Gen. Mgr.)
                          7871-136
IBM Communications Systems (1)
P.O. Box 100, Rte. 100
Somers, NY 10589
Tel.: 914-766-1900
Devel. & Mfr. of Computer Communication
Products; Controllers, Modems, Connectivity
& Network Mgmnt. Software
S.I.C.: 3577; 7372
Ellen M. Hancock (V.P. & Gen. Mgr.)
                          7871-137
IBM Enterprise Systems (1)
P.O. Box 100, Rte. 100
Somers, NY 10589
Tel.: 914-766-1900
Advanced Computers, Processors &
Subsystems; High-Volume Printers & Software
Products
S.I.C.: 3571; 3577; 7372
Carl J. Conti, Sr. (V.P. & Gen. Mgr.)
                          7871-138
IBM Personal Systems (1)
44 S. Broadway
White Plains, NY 10601
Tel.: 914-686-1900
Desktop Computer Systems, Software,
Supplies & Printers
S.I.C.: 3571; 3577; 7372
R.T. Gerstner (V.P. & Gen. Mgr.)
                          7871-139
IBM Programming Systems (1)
2000 Purchase St.
Purchase, NY 10577
Tel.: 914-697-6000
Develops Data Management Software,
Programming Languages & Application
Development Software
S.I.C.: 7372
Earl F. Wheeler (V.P. & Gen. Mgr.)
                          7871-140
IBM Technology Products (1)
1000 Westchester Ave.
White Plains, NY 10604
Tel.: 914-696-1900
Devel. & Mfg. of Logic & Memory Technology
& Electronic Packaging
S.I.C.: 3571; 3572
Patrick A. Toole (Sr. V.P. & Gen. Mgr.)
                          7871-002
IBM Systems Integration Div. (1)
6600 Rockledge Dr.
Bethesda, MD 20817
Tel.: 301-493-8100
Provides Information-Handling & Control
Systems to Federal Govt. for Seaborne,
Spaceborne, Airborne & Ground-Based
Environments; Participates in Applied
Research & Exploratory Devel.
S.I.C.: 7379
Gerald W. Ebker (V.P.)

                          7871-013
IBM Real Estate & Construction Div.
(1)
208 Harbor Dr.
Stamford, CT 06904
Tel.: 203-352-7000
Manages Selection & Acquisition of Sites,
Design & Construction of Bldgs. & Purchase
& Lease of Facilities for all IBM Opers. in
U.S.
S.I.C.: 6531
Arthur J. Hedges, Jr. (V.P.)
                          7871-014
IBM Research Div. (1)
P.O. Box 218
Yorktown Heights, NY 10598
Tel.: 914-945-3000
Brings Scientific Understanding to Bear on
Areas of Co. Interest Through Basic
Research & the Devel. of Technologies of
Potential Long-Range Importance
S.I.C.: 8731
John A. Armstrong (V.P.-Science &
Technology)

Independent Business Units:
                          7871-015
IBM Credit Corporation (1)
290 Harbor Dr.
Stamford, CT 06904
Tel.: 203-352-5100
Finances Installment Payment Agreements
S.I.C.: 6153
Harry L. Kavetas (Pres.)
                          7871-017
IBM World Trade Europe/Middle East/
Africa Corp. (1)
900 King St.
Rye Brook, NY 10573
Tel.: 914-934-4000
Provides Designated Support to World Trade
Organizational Units
S.I.C.: 3577; 3579
C. Michael Armstrong (Pres.)
                          7871-018
IBM World Trade Americas Group (1)
Rte. 9, Town of Mount Pleasant
North Tarrytown, NY 10591
Tel.: 914-332-2000
Conducts IBM's Business in 26 Countries in
the Western Hemisphere
S.I.C.: 3577
James J. Forese (V.P. & Grp. Exec.)

Subsidiary:
                          7871-024
ROLM Company (1)
P.O. Box 5017
Norwalk, CT 06856-5017
Tel.: 203-849-6000
Approx. Sls.: $900,000,000
Emp: 11,500
Fiscal Year-end: 12/31/88
ROLM Products & Siemens Private Network
Communications
S.I.C.: 3661
H. Mitchell Watson (Pres. & Chief Exec.
Officer)

Division:
                          7871-026
ROLM Systems (2)
4900 Old Ironsides Dr.
Santa Clara, CA 95050
Devel. & Mfg. of PBX Systems, Telephones &
Other Telecommunications Products
S.I.C.: 3661
Ray S. AbuZayyad (Pres. & Chief Exec.
Officer)

Joint Venture:
                          7871-126
Prodigy Services Company (1)
445 Hamilton Ave.
White Plains, NY 10601
Tel.: 914-993-8000   (50%)
Commercial Videotex Services for Persons
with Home or Personal Computers; Joint
Venture of IBM and Sears, Roebuck & Co.
S.I.C.: 7379
Theodore Papes (Pres.)

† *   7874-000

INTERNATIONAL DAIRY
QUEEN, INC.
5701 Green Valley Dr.
Minneapolis, MN 55437
Mailing Address: P. O. Box
35286
Minneapolis, MN 55435
Tel.: 612-830-0200   DE
Telefax: 612-830-0270
Year Founded: 1962
INDQ—(OTC)

580

† Refer to the International Directory of Corporate Affiliations for information about foreign holdings.

Reprinted by permission from *Directory of Corporate Affiliations*, 1990 edition.

We are also told that in 1987 its revenues were $54.22 billion.
It has 396,000 employees.
It is on the New York Stock Exchange, among others.
We are told that its products are: information processing products and systems, etc.
We are given SIC numbers. These are numbers assigned by the federal government to all industries. Because they make it simple to tag specific types of businesses, Standard Industrial Classification numbers are used by many nongovernment organizations as well.

Dun & Bradstreet's *Million Dollar Directory* supplies almost identical information about any company. *Thomas Register of American Manufacturers* gives you at least the name, address, and telephone number and type of business of a manufacturer. Sometimes *Thomas* lists branch offices, subsidiaries, and officers' names. It's a good place to look if you don't find the company in either of the other two books just mentioned.

International Business Machines has divisions all over the country. If you'd like to know where in the United States you might be sent, you could check either the *Directory of Corporate Affiliations* (Figure 3-2) or *America's Corporate Families: The Billion Dollar Directory*. In either of these publications, you will find somewhat detailed information about the related branches of the company.

Financial Rankings

At this point, you know some basic things about IBM. It would take about fifteen minutes to find out this much once you got to the library.

FIGURE 3-3. Top thirteen Fortune 500 companies.

RANK		COMPANY	SALES		PROFITS			ASSETS		STOCKHOLDER EQUITY	
1988	1987		$ Millions	% change from 1987	$ Millions	Rank	% change from 1987	$ Millions	Rank	$ Millions	Rank
1	1	GENERAL MOTORS Detroit	121,085.4	19.0	4,856.3	4	36.8	164,063.1	1	35,671.7	2
2	3	FORD MOTOR Dearborn, Mich.	92,445.6	29.0	5,300.2	2	14.6	143,366.5	2	21,529.0	4
3	2	EXXON New York	79,557.0*	4.1	5,260.0	3	8.7	74,293.0	4	31,767.0	3
4	4	INT'L BUSINESS MACHINES Armonk, N.Y.	59,681.0	10.1	5,806.0	1	10.4	73,037.0	5	39,509.0	1
5	6	GENERAL ELECTRIC Fairfield, Conn.¹	49,414.0	25.7	3,386.0	5	16.2	110,865.0	3	18,466.0	5
6	5	MOBIL New York	48,198.0*	(5.9)	2,087.0	9	65.9	38,820.0	7	15,686.0	6
7	10	CHRYSLER Highland Park, Mich.	35,472.7	35.1	1,050.2	21	(18.6)	48,566.8	6	7,582.3	13
8	7	TEXACO White Plains, N.Y.	33,544.0*	(2.4)	1,304.0	17	—	26,337.0	14	8,105.0	11
9	9	E.I. DU PONT DE NEMOURS Wilmington, Del.	32,514.0*	6.7	2,190.0	8	22.6	30,719.0	10	15,580.0	7
10	12	PHILIP MORRIS New York²	25,860.0*	16.1	2,337.0	7	26.9	36,960.0	8	7,679.0	12
11	11	CHEVRON San Francisco	25,196.0*	(3.1)	1,768.0	11	75.6	33,968.0	9	14,788.0	9
12	14	AMOCO Chicago	21,150.0*	4.8	2,063.0	10	51.7	29,919.0	11	13,342.0	10
13	13	SHELL OIL Houston³	21,070.0*	1.0	1,239.0	18	0.7	27,169.0	12	15,381.0	8

Because a company's overall effectiveness depends greatly on its financial strength, you will want to know as much as possible about that aspect of the companies you are researching. How well a corporation will be able to meet its debts, attract investors, produce a product or service, support research and development, hire and keep good people, even stay in business, will be strongly influenced by its financial situation.

Financial statements present evidence about past and present strength and give indications about the future. If your coursework has never included financial analysis, you may want to do some reading on your own to gain some understanding of the contents of financial statements. Numerous guides exist for that purpose. A particularly good introduction to reading financial statements is Merrill Lynch's *How To Read a Financial Report*.

One of the easiest ways to get clues about the relative financial strengths of the largest U.S. corporations is by using *Fortune* and *Forbes* magazines. Both *Fortune* and *Forbes* magazines compare the large companies each year. You can either refer to the separate issues of *Fortune* listing the various groups ranked each year or use *The Fortune Directory*, an annual compilation of these lists.

Looking at *The Fortune Directory*'s entry for IBM, (Figure 3-3) we can see that in 1988 IBM ranked fourth in sales but first in net income among all the Fortune 500 largest U.S. industrial corporations. In earnings per share, it improved over the ten years from 1978 to 1988, but in total return to investors in 1988, it ranked 250 among the Fortune 500. In other measures of profitability, net income as a percentage of sales, net income as a percentage of assets, and net income as a percentage of stockholders' equity, it ranked 87th, 171st, and 256th, respectively.

| MARKET VALUE | | PROFITS AS PERCENT OF | | | | | | EARNINGS PER SHARE | | | | TOTAL RETURN TO INVESTORS | | | | INDUSTRY TABLE NUMBER | RANK |
| | | SALES | | ASSETS | | STOCKHOLDERS' EQUITY | | | % change from 1987 | 1978-88 annual growth rate | | 1988 | | 1978-88 annual average | | | |
$ Millions	Rank	%	Rank	%	Rank	%	Rank	1988/$		%	Rank	%	Rank	%	Rank		1988
25,773.8	5	4.0	299	3.0	382	13.6	286	7.17	42.5	1.6	291	45.1	61	11.6	289	17	1
24,552.8	7	5.7	210	3.7	357	24.6	65	10.96	21.1	14.0	90	40.4	70	24.3	74	17	2
57,130.1	2	6.6	167	7.1	204	16.6	213	3.95	15.2	9.8	168	21.1	166	22.1	99	18	3
70,056.6	1	9.7	87	7.9	171	14.7	256	9.80	12.4	6.3	223	9.6	250	9.8	312	6	4
40,595.2	3	6.9	157	3.1	379	18.3	172	3.75	17.2	10.8	152	4.8	298	19.0	152	7	5
19,971.7	10	4.3	283	5.4	284	13.3	292	5.07	65.7	6.7	216	22.5	158	17.4	193	18	6
6,269.1	45	3.0	353	2.2	394	13.9	279	4.66	(21.0)	—		21.3	165	23.1	87	17	7
12,771.2	23	3.9	308	5.0	315	16.1	221	5.35	—	5.5	239	43.6	64	16.1	216	18	8
23,491.1	8	6.7	160	7.1	202	14.1	272	9.11	23.3	5.4	243	5.5	289	13.7	256	5	9
26,911.5	4	9.0	102	6.3	238	30.4	40	10.03	29.4	19.5	32	24.4	143	24.1	78	25	10
17,704.2	12	7.0	153	5.2	296	12.0	317	5.17	75.9	4.8	248	21.9	161	13.3	262	18	11
20,811.9	9	9.8	86	6.9	213	15.5	239	4.00	50.7	8.1	190	13.8	218	16.2	213	18	12
N.A.		5.9	198	4.6	330	8.1	366	—	—	—		—		—		18	13

Another popular source of comparative information about corporations is *Value Line* (Figure 3-4). In addition to examining individual companies, *Value Line* analyzes their industries. For a specific corporation, *Value Line* gives financial information—some of it going back 16 years: revenues per share, earnings per share, revenues, net profit, long-term debt ratio, etc. It also provides some projections into the near future. You can do your own analysis of the figures presented here, but down at the bottom of the page in the right hand corner, *Value Line* gives IBM an A++ rating for financial strength.

Another particularly good source of comparative information is *Standard & Poor's Industry Surveys* (Figure 3-5). There we find a text about the computer and office equipment industry and a statistical picture of the companies in this group. IBM and its competitors are shown as a group with current data on revenues, net income, return on assets, return on equity, etc., some ratio analysis and historical data as well.

As you might expect, every day there are many articles published on various industries and companies in periodicals. They too offer comparative information. You can find articles by looking in the *Predicasts F&S Index United States* under the name of the company or by industry or you can look in the indexes to the *Wall Street Journal* or the *New York Times* or the *National Newspaper Index* to find articles published in the newspapers. *Business Index* will give you access to periodical articles as well as articles in the financial section of the *New York Times* and the *Wall Street Journal*. Corporate names also appear in *Business Periodicals Index* if you want to use that to find articles in business journals.

Forbes magazine publishes an "Annual Report on American Industry" in its first January issue. There you will find comparative information indicating the rank of a company in a number of categories such as return on equity, return on total capital, and sales growth. The computer industry, as well as a wide range of other industries, is included there. Another source of comparative information is *Business Week's* "Scoreboard Special" which appears in March each year.

Using *Predicasts F&S Index United States* and looking at its white pages, you may find information about a specific company. *Predicasts F&S Index United States* also gives access to articles on industries.

Biographical Information

We have heard it said that an institution is often the lengthened shadow of a person. That can be very true of some corporations. The person at the top of a company is frequently a good example of what the company as a whole values in its people. Sometimes by studying the lives and careers of the top people in a company, you can get something of an idea of how you might fit in.

FIGURE 3-4. Sample page from *Value Line*.

| INT'L BUS. MACH. NYSE-IBM | RECENT PRICE | 113 | P/E RATIO | 11.0 (Trailing: 11.3 Median: 12.8) | RELATIVE P/E RATIO | 0.85 | DIV'D YLD | 4.3% | VALUE LINE | 1098 |

TIMELINESS 3 Average (Relative Price Performance Next 12 Mos.)

SAFETY 1 Highest (Scale: 1 Highest to 5 Lowest)

BETA .95 (1.00 = Market)

1992-94 PROJECTIONS

	Price	Gain	Ann'l Total Return
High	220	(+95%)	20%
Low	180	(+60%)	15%

Insider Decisions

	O	N	D	J	F	M	A	M	J
to Buy	0	0	0	0	0	0	1	1	0
Options	0	2	4	0	4	0	0	0	3
to Sell	0	0	0	0	2	0	1	0	0

Institutional Decisions

	3Q'88	4Q'88	1Q'89
to Buy	192	191	193
to Sell	260	215	266
Hld's(000)	276874	263686	275171

Percent shares traded: 9.0 6.0 3.0

Target Price Range 1992 1993 1994 1995

High: 80.5 72.8 71.5 98.0 134.3 128.5 158.8 161.9 175.9 129.5 130.9
Low: 61.1 50.4 48.4 55.6 92.3 99.0 117.4 119.3 102.0 104.5 106.3

8.0 x "Cash Flow" p sh
4-for-1 split
Relative Price Strength
Options: CBOE

1974	1975	1976	1977	1978	1979	1980	1981	1982	1983	1984	1985	1986	1987	1988	1989	1990	1991	© VALUE LINE, INC.	92-94E	
21.37	24.09	27.05	30.74	36.14	39.18	44.90	49.08	57.04	65.79	74.96	81.34	84.49	90.77	100.78	110.35	117.65		Revenues per sh	166.65	
5.75	6.12	6.83	7.67	8.88	9.14	10.83	11.21	13.23	15.43	15.99	15.61	14.47	16.15	17.94	19.05	20.55		"Cash Flow" per sh	29.20	
3.12	3.34	3.99	4.58	5.32	5.16	6.10	5.63	7.39	9.04	10.77	10.67	7.81	8.72	9.83	10.25	11.00		Earnings per sh A	16.50	
1.39	1.63	2.00	2.50	2.88	3.44	3.44	3.44	3.44	3.71	4.10	4.40	4.40	4.40	4.40	4.73	5.00		Div'ds Decl'd per sh B	7.00	
4.69	3.83	3.94	5.43	6.51	9.66	10.61	11.56	11.10	8.07	8.93	10.45	7.62	7.21	9.14	10.15	12.10		Cap'l Spending per sh	15.00	
17.05	19.05	21.15	21.39	23.14	25.64	28.18	30.66	33.13	38.02	43.23	51.98	56.67	64.06	66.96	71.65	77.35		Book Value per sh	100.55	
593.04	599.38	602.78	589.88	583.24	583.59	583.81	592.29	602.41	610.72	612.69	615.42	606.61	597.33	590.04	580.00	578.00		Common Shs Outst'g C	578.00	
16.5	15.3	16.6	14.5	12.7	13.9	10.4	10.3	9.4	12.7	10.8	12.3	18.0	16.6	11.9	Bold figures are Value Line estimates			Avg Ann'l P/E Ratio	12.0	
2.31	2.04	2.12	1.90	1.73	2.01	1.38	1.25	1.04	1.07	1.01	1.00	1.22	1.11	.99				Relative P/E Ratio	1.00	
2.7%	3.2%	3.0%	3.8%	4.3%	4.8%	5.4%	5.9%	5.0%	3.2%	3.5%	3.4%	3.1%	3.0%	3.8%				Avg Ann'l Div'd Yield	3.5%	

CAPITAL STRUCTURE as of 3/31/89 F
Total Debt $13807 mill. Due in 5 Yrs $9974 mill.
LT Debt $8888 mill.   LT Interest $774.0 mill.
Incl. $1254 mill. 7 7/8% sub. debs. ('04) cv. into 6.51 com. shs. at $153.6563. Redeemable at 104.725% in 11/68 and at decreasing prices thereafter. Sinking fund pmts. begin 1994.
(Total interest coverage: 13.5x) (19% of Cap'l)
Leases, Uncapitalized: Annual rentals $1341.0 mill.
Pension Liability None in '88 vs. None in '87
Pfd Stock None
Common Stock 582,726,135 shs.   (81% of Cap'l)
(590.9 mill. fully diluted shs.)
as of 4/30/89

CURRENT POSITION	1987	1988 F	3/31/89
Cash Assets	6967	5123	3879
Receivables	13649	18100	15599
Inventory(Avg Cst)	8645	9565	9617
Other	1559	1555	3984
Current Assets	31020	35343	33079
Accts Payable	2627	2702	2265
Debt Due	1629	4862	4919
Other	9121	9823	8233
Current Liab.	13377	17387	15417

ANNUAL RATES of change (per sh)	Past 10 Yrs.	Past 5 Yrs.	Est'd '86-'88 to '92-'94
Revenue	11.5%	10.0%	10.5%
"Cash Flow"	7.5%	4.0%	10.5%
Earnings	6.5%	3.5%	11.0%
Dividends	6.0%	4.5%	8.0%
Book Value	11.0%	13.0%	8.0%

Calendar	QUARTERLY REVENUES ($ mill.) F				Full Year
	Mar.31	June 30	Sep.30	Dec.31	
1986	10127	12268	11910	16945	51250
1987	10681	12798	12727	18011	54217
1988	12058	13907	13714	19782	59461
1989	12730	15213	14050	21207	64000
1990	13000	16500	16300	21400	68000

Calendar	EARNINGS PER SHARE A				Full Year
	Mar.31	June 30	Sep.30	Dec.31	
1986	1.65	2.12	1.76	2.28	7.81
1987	1.30	1.95	2.00	3.47	8.72
1988	1.57	2.14	2.10	4.02	9.83
1989	1.61	2.31	2.20	4.13	10.25
1990	1.75	2.50	2.35	4.40	11.00

Calendar	QUARTERLY DIVIDENDS PAID B ■				Full Year
	Mar.31	June 30	Sep.30	Dec.31	
1985	1.10	1.10	1.10	1.10	4.40
1986	1.10	1.10	1.10	1.10	4.40
1987	1.10	1.10	1.10	1.10	4.40
1988	1.10	1.10	1.10	1.10	4.40
1989	1.10	1.21			

						26213	29070	34364	40180	45937	50056	51250	54217	59461	64000	68000		Revenues ($mill) F	95000
						32.4%	32.2%	33.8%	33.7%	31.4%	28.5%	23.1%	22.4%	23.8%	24.0%	24.0%		Operating Margin	24.0%
						2759.0	3329.0	3562.0	3938.0	3215.0	3051.0	3988.0	4390.0	4764.0	5075	5500		Depreciation ($mill) D	7175
						3562.0	3308.0	4409.0	5485.0	6582.0	6555.0	4789.0	5258.0	5824.0	5305	6375		Net Profit ($mill)	9455
						39.6%	44.8%	44.4%	44.8%	43.4%	43.6%	42.9%	38.9%	39.2%	41.5%	41.0%		Income Tax Rate	40.0%
						13.6%	11.4%	12.8%	13.7%	14.3%	13.1%	9.3%	9.7%	9.8%	9.4%	9.4%		Net Profit Margin	10.0%
						3399.0	2983.0	4805.0	7763.0	10735	14637	15006	17643	17956	18750	23000		Working Cap'l ($mill)	22575
						2099.0	2669.0	2851.0	2674.0	3269.0	3955.0	4169.0	3858.0	8518.0	8650	8500		Long-Term Debt ($mill)	8500
						16453	18161	19960	23219	26489	31990	34374	38263	39509	41500	44700		Net Worth ($mill)	57325
						19.8%	16.5%	20.0%	21.7%	22.7%	18.8%	12.9%	12.9%	12.9%	12.5%	12.5%		% Earned Total Cap'l	15.0%
						21.6%	18.2%	22.1%	23.6%	24.8%	20.5%	13.9%	13.7%	14.7%	14.5%	14.5%		% Earned Net Worth	16.5%
						9.4%	7.1%	11.8%	13.9%	15.4%	12.0%	6.1%	6.8%	8.1%	8.0%	8.0%		% Retained to Comm Eq	9.5%
						56%	61%	47%	41%	38%	41%	56%	50%	45%	46%	45%		% All Div'ds to Net Prof	42%

BUSINESS: International Business Machines Corporation is the largest supplier of advanced information processing and communication systems and services, and program products. Also makes typewriters. 1988 revenue breakdown: Sales, 67%; support services, 16%; software, 13%; Rentals and financing 4%. Foreign business accounted for 58% of 1988 revenues, 74% of pretax earnings. Research, development and engineering costs equaled 9.9% of revenues. '88 depreciation rate: 10.6%. Estimated plant age: 5 years. Has 387,110 employees, 833,785 shareholders. Insiders control .6% of stock. Chairman and Chief Executive Officer: John Akers. President: J.D. Kuehler. Inc.: New York. Address: Armonk, NY 10504. Tel.: 914-765-1900.

Things are looking up for IBM in 1989. June-quarter sales were good worldwide, rising at a double-digit rate both in the U.S. and overseas (measured in local currencies), and across the product line. The stronger dollar did trim 20¢ a share from the period's earnings. But helped by a nearly 2% reduction in shares outstanding, share net advanced by nearly 8%. We are looking for gains in the next two quarters as well. Price cutting to win sales in the face of fierce competition probably will keep margins tight in the mainframe line. However, we expect continued strong demand for personal computers and midrange machines. Currency translation effects likely will again trim earnings a bit in the September and December interims, though, and Value Line forecasts slowing economic growth as the year wears down. So, on balance, we've pared our estimate of IBM's full-year earnings by 40¢ a share, to $10.25.

Big Blue appears to be poised for faster growth in the early years of the next decade. Starting in late 1990 or early '91, mainframe sales should benefit as production of the next-generation Summit ramps up. Tools that ease the migration of applications from older *System 36s* to the *AS/400* probably will keep the newer midrange machines selling briskly. And sales of the *PS/2* line of personal computers should be helped as software that more fully utilizes the capabilities of its powerful central processor becomes available. Finally, we think IBM's efforts to tie its product families together so data and resources can be shared throughout the enterprise will solidify its position in large accounts and improve sales all up and down the line.

These shares are worth more than a passing glance, although they are only ranked 3, Average, for relative price appreciation during the next six to 12 months. The earnings gains we're projecting for the early Nineties appear to be sufficient to allow the issue to at least track the market during the 3 to 5 years ahead, and to fuel further dividend hikes: Thus, total returns to 1992-94 should be well above average. Moreover, the top-notch Safety rank and Financial Strength rating make this equity suitable for most accounts.
George A. Niemond   *August 4, 1989*

(A) Based on average shares outstanding. Excludes nonrecurring gains (losses): '88, 86¢, (89¢). Next earnings report due mid-Oct. (B) Next dividend meeting about Oct. 25. Goes ex about Nov. 3. Dividend payment dates: about March 10, June 10, Sept. 10, Dec. 10. ■ Dividend reinvestment plan available (no brokerage fee). (C) In millions, adjusted for stock splits and dividends. (D) Depreciation on accelerated basis. (E) Fully diluted 3- to 5-years hence. (F) Includes fin. subsidiary from 1988.

Company's Financial Strength	A++
Stock's Price Stability	95
Price Growth Persistence	40
Earnings Predictability	70

Factual material is obtained from sources believed to be reliable, but the publisher is not responsible for any errors or omissions contained herein.

FIGURE 3-5.   Sample entry from Standard & Poor's *Industry Surveys*.

STANDARD&POOR'S

industry surveys

● 1989 Standard & Poor's Corporation   USPS No. 517-780

JUNE 15, 1989 (Vol. 157, No. 24, Sec. 3)

Replaces Basic Analysis dated Oct. 1, 1987

computers &
office equipment
BASIC ANALYSIS

FIGURE 3-5. Sample entry from Standard & Poor's *Industry Surveys*.

1988 MARKET SHARES—PERSONAL COMPUTERS
(U.S. Vendors' Shares of Worldwide Value of Shipments)

IBM 27.9%
Other 41.2%
Apple 12.2%
Compaq 8.3%
Tandy 5.0%
Zenith 5.4%

Source: Dataquest Inc.

on the 16-bit *80286* microprocessor became available and sales skyrocketed; two years of relatively slow growth followed. In 1987, products based on INTEL's 32-bit *80386* chip, such as IBM's new line of personal computers—the *PS/2* family—were introduced, and APPLE upgraded its product line with systems based on MOTOROLA's *68030* microprocessor. Buyers need time to assimilate their purchases, to figure out what they've got, what they need, and where they're going with distributed data processing. The *80486* was introduced by INTEL in April 1989, but products based on this microprocessor are not expected until 1990. Indeed, next year could be when PC sales return to very rapid growth. In the meantime, however, the market suddenly has become extremely confusing. Whereas the PC industry always stood on the firm bedrock of standards, i.e., *DOS* and the INTEL microprocessor family, now it is fraught with choices.

Muscling in on IBM's action

Faced with slowing PC growth and continuously declining market share, IBM did some soul-searching in the mid-1980s. Having designed its original PC to be made of cheap and widely available off-the-shelf components and to run MICROSOFT's *DOS* operating system, IBM didn't have a lock in the PC market the way it did with proprietary mainframes and minicomputers. Although it continued to provide the pricing umbrella for the industry, its PC margins were still well below its mainframes', and PCs were increasing as a percentage of total sales. Further, it was becoming clear that the world was moving away from mainframes to workstations and PCs, whether IBM liked it or not. In April 1987, IBM annoyed the computer world by bucking the industry trend towards standards when it introduced *PS/2*, its new line of personal computers. *PS/2* is based on a proprietary architecture called the Micro Channel Architecture (MCA), a 32-bit bus structure which IBM indicated it would vigorously defend in the courts. (A bus is the channel, or path, for transferring data, in this case between the computer and peripherals.) While saying that it would willingly license the technology, the licensing fees of up to 5% of product cost—in an industry where gross margins can be less than 40%—smacked of highway robbery. In addition, IBM was seeking back royalties of up to 1% for machines sold prior to

the new policy. And, more importantly, IBM would control who its competitors would be. Big Blue may have shot itself in the foot.

When it became clear a year and a half after its introduction that IBM's MCA bus was not yet a raging success, COMPAQ, IBM's nemesis, and eight other major computer vendors—HEWLETT-PACKARD, TANDY, AST TECHNOLOGY, NEC, ZENITH, EPSON, WYSE, and OLIVETTI—banded together in September 1988 to surround this Big Blue Alamo. The Gang of Nine announced their own alternative bus structure, the Extended Industry Standard Architecture (EISA). Additional support came from MICROSOFT and INTEL. EISA products are expected in late 1989.

Undoubtedly, there was a need for a higher performance bus structure: the old AT-bus, moving data in 16-bit increments, was resulting in an information-flow bottleneck; the new *80386* machines process in 32-bit increments. But by redesigning the bus structure, IBM rendered a substantial portion of its installed base of peripherals obsolete. IBM countered that most peripheral add-in boards are primarily designed to upgrade old machines and therefore are rarely migrated to new machines, i.e., MCA systems, where that additional functionality is already built in. An arguable point, but the company committed the gaffe of appearing to try to bend the industry to its will, and away from the standard AT-bus. Customers simply do not want proprietary systems.

Although a handful of vendors, including TANDY and DELL COMPUTER, announced their intent to manufacture MCA clones in early 1988, demand never really materialized, and little has been heard on this front since. Some blame the lack of clones for *PS/2*'s slow start. Most of the demand for the MCA products came from Fortune 500 companies that traditionally buy IBM and wanted products that would conform to IBM's SAA strategy, which, when implemented, will facilitate communication across IBM's diverse products. IBM says it has shipped over 3 million *PS/2*s. The *PS/2* is likely to be a succesful product, if only because it is an IBM, but it will take time to bear fruit. Interest is high, but, according to a Datamation survey taken last year, users don't see a need to switch over immediately. Furthermore, IBM had some production problems, most of which were solved by May 1989.

Confusion reigns supreme in the market. With the proliferation of PCs and continued incorporation of ease-of-use features, PC buyers are not necessarily very sophisticated technologically. They don't want to know what a bus is, let alone choose one. The feud between IBM and the Gang of Nine has reawakened memories of the bad old days when a buyer could not be assured of true IBM-compatibility and all too often got a machine home only to discover that it would not run a popular off-the-shelf software program. Fortunately, software compatibility is not at issue here, but that is not well understood. MICROSOFT is supporting both architectures with its *OS/2* operating system. Since applications run under the operating system, if a package is compatible with *OS/2* for MCA, it will also run on an *OS/2* for EISA. It will make a difference when buying peripherals and add-in boards, but the list of suppliers supporting both MCA and EISA is very long. Eventually, the market will decide for itself which will dominate. There probably will be two standards. Life would be easy if these were the only two scenarios, but the choices don't stop there.

DOS, OS/2, or *Unix*

Suddenly, instead of one, we have three operating systems to choose from for our *80386*-based personal computers.

FIGURE 3-5.   Sample entry from Standard & Poor's *Industry Surveys*.

COMPARATIVE COMPANY ANALYSIS — Computers & Office Equipment

Company	Yr. End	Operating Revenues — Million $							Compound Growth Rate (%)			Index Basis (1978 = 100)				
		1978	1983	1984	1985	1986	1987	1988	1-Yr.	5-Yr.	10-Yr.	1984	1985	1986	1987	1988
COMPUTER SYSTEM MANUFACTURERS																
ALLIANT COMPUTER SYSTEMS CP	DEC	NA	NA	NA	4.4	30.8	53.8	84.8A	20.5	NA	NA	NA	..	..	..	..
ALTOS COMPUTER SYS	JUN	NA	74.8	102.7	124.4	134.2	153.9	175.9	14.2	18.7	NA	NA	..	..	..	..
AMDAHL CORP	DEC	320.9	777.7	779.4	862.0	966.3	1505.2	1801.8	19.7	18.3	18.8	243	269	301	469	561
APOLLO COMPUTER INC	DEC	NA	80.7	215.9	295.6	391.7	553.7	653.5	18.0	52.0	NA	NA	..	..	..	..
CONTROL DATA CORP	DEC	1846.4	4582.8	5026.9	3679.7D	3346.7	3366.5	3628.3	7.8	-4.8	7.0	272	199	181	182	197
CONVEX COMPUTER CORP	DEC	NA	NA	NA	13.5	40.2	69.6	105.6	51.6	NA	NA	NA	..	..	..	..
CRAY RESEARCH	DEC	17.2	169.7	228.8	380.2	596.7	687.3	756.3	10.0	34.8	46.0	1332	2213	3474	4002	4403
DATA GENERAL CORP	SEP	379.9	828.9	1160.8	1239.0	1268.0A	1274.3C	1364.7	7.1	10.5	13.6	306	326	334	336	359
DATAPOINT CORP	JUL	162.3	540.2	600.2	520.2	325.2	312.1	330.8	6.0	-9.3	7.4	370	321	200	192	204
DIGITAL EQUIPMENT	JUN	1436.6	4271.8	5584.4	6686.3	7590.3	9389.4	11475.4	22.2	21.9	23.1	389	465	528	654	799
FLOATING POINT SYSTEMS INC	OCT	25.3	100.2	118.4	126.6	88.6	84.3	70.8	-16.0	-6.7	10.8	467	500	350	333	279
HEWLETT-PACKARD CO	OCT	1728.0	4710.0	6044.0C	6505.0	7102.0	8090.0	9831.0	21.5	15.9	19.0	350	376	411	468	569
INTERGRAPH CORP	DEC	NA	252.0	403.8	526.4	605.7	641.1	800.2	24.8	26.0	NA	NA	..	..	..	..
INTL BUSINESS MACHINES CORP	DEC	21076.1	40180.0	45937.0	50056.0	51250.0	54217.0	59681.0C	10.1	8.2	11.0	218	238	243	257	283
MAI BASIC FOUR INC	SEP	NA	NA	NA	168.5	281.0	321.0A	420.8A	31.1	NA	NA	NA	..	..	..	..
NBI INC	JUN	NA	120.9	177.1	216.7A	282.4	278.3	137.7D	-50.5	2.6	NA	NA	..	..	..	..
NCR CORP	DEC	2610.5D	3730.9	4074.3	4317.2	4881.6	5640.7	5989.9	6.2	9.9	8.7	156	165	187	216	229
PRIME COMPUTER	DEC	93.6	516.5	642.8	769.7	860.2	960.9A	1594.6A	65.9	25.3	32.8	687	823	919	1027	1704
SILICON GRAPHICS INC	JUN	NA	NA	NA	NA	41.5	86.3	152.6	76.9	NA	NA	NA	..	..	..	..
STRATUS COMPUTER INC	DEC	NA	20.6	42.1	80.2	124.6	184.2	265.3	44.1	66.8	NA	NA	..	..	..	..
SUN MICROSYSTEMS INC	JUN	NA	NA	NA	115.2	210.1	537.5A	1051.6A	95.6	NA	NA	NA	..	..	..	..
TANDEM COMPUTERS INC	SEP	24.3	418.3	532.6	624.1	767.8	1035.5	1314.7A	27.0	25.7	49.0	2191	2568	3159	4260	5409
UNISYS CORP	DEC	2422.3	4298.5	4808.3	5037.1	7432.4A	9712.9	9902.0	1.9	18.2	15.1	199	208	307	401	409
WANG LABORATORIES -CL B	JUN	198.0	1538.0	2184.7	2351.7	2642.5	2836.7C	3068.4	8.2	14.8	31.5	1104	1188	1335	1433	1550
PERIPHERAL EQUIPMENT AND SUBSYSTEMS																
DATAPRODUCTS CORP	MAR	163.6	398.6A	471.8	353.8	338.8A	345.2	NA	NA	NA	NA	288	216	207	211	NA
EKCO GROUP INC	DEC	73.3	164.1	171.5	216.3	2.2D	25.9A	134.8	421.2	-3.9	6.3	234	295	3	35	184
MSI ELECTRONICS INC	SEP	NA	2.1	2.3	2.5	2.5	1.5	1.4	-6.0	-7.6	NA	NA	NA	NA	NA	NA
MEMOREX TELEX CORP	MAR	142.7	318.3	591.0A	695.0	821.9	880.5	NA	NA	NA	NA	414	487	576	617	NA
OANTEL CORP	APR	178.3A	402.5	362.9	236.7	65.8	58.2	NA	NA	NA	NA	204	133	37	33	NA
RECOGNITION EQUIPMENT INC	OCT	86.7	117.0	140.1A	163.1A	241.8	264.7	260.8A	-1.5	17.4	11.6	162	188	279	305	301
STORAGE TECHNOLOGY CORP	DEC	300.4	886.6D	808.6	673.4C	696.0	750.0	874.0	16.5	-0.3	11.3	269	224	232	250	291
SUMMAGRAPHICS CORP	MAY	NA	NA	NA	NA	28.5	35.8	NA	NA	NA	NA	NA	..	..	..	..
PERSONAL COMPUTERS																
APPLE COMPUTER INC	SEP	NA	982.8	1515.9	1918.3	1901.9	2661.1	4071.4	53.0	32.9	NA	NA	..	..	..	..
COMMODORE INTL LTD	JUN	50.2A	681.2	1267.2	883.1	889.3	806.7	871.1	8.0	5.0	33.0	2527	1761	1773	1609	1737
COMPAQ COMPUTER CORP	DEC	NA	111.2	329.0	503.9	625.2	1224.1	2065.6	68.7	79.4	NA	NA	..	..	..	..
DELL COMPUTER CORP	JAN	NA	NA	NA	NA	NA	159.0	257.8	62.1	NA	NA	NA	..	..	..	..
TANDY CORP	JUN	1059.3	2475.2	2737.0	2841.4	3036.0	3452.2	3793.8	9.9	8.9	13.6	258	268	287	326	358
COMPUTER SOFTWARE																
ASHTON-TATE CO	JAN	NA	43.0	82.3	121.8A,C	210.8A	267.3	307.3	14.9	48.2	NA	NA	..	..	..	..
AUTODESK INC	JAN	NA	NA	9.9	29.5	52.4	79.3	117.3A	48.0	NA	NA	NA	..	..	..	..
COMPUTER ASSOCIATES INTL INC	MAR	NA	84.7A	128.9A	191.0A	309.3A	709.1A	NA	NA	NA	NA	NA	..	..	..	..
CULINET SOFTWARE INC	APR	13.9A	120.0	184.1	184.3	174.9A	216.7	NA	NA	NA	NA	1322	1323	1256	1556	NA
INFORMIX CORP	DEC	NA	NA	NA	10.6	21.1	41.6	103.5A	148.7	NA	NA	NA	..	..	..	..
LEGENT CORP	SEP	NA	4.8	7.5	11.1	24.2	37.7	50.3	33.5	60.0	NA	NA	..	..	..	..
LOTUS DEVELOPMENT CORP	DEC	NA	53.0	157.0	225.5A	282.9	395.6	468.5	18.4	54.8	NA	NA	..	..	..	..
MANAGEMENT SCIENCE AMERICA	DEC	NA	139.1	141.8A,C	151.7	193.4A	258.5C	250.0	-3.3	12.4	NA	NA	..	..	..	..
MICROSOFT CORP	JUN	NA	NA	NA	140.4	197.5	345.9	590.8	70.8	NA	NA	NA	..	..	..	..
MICROPRO INTL	AUG	NA	43.8	66.9	42.6	38.2	41.3	42.5	2.7	-0.6	NA	NA	..	..	..	..
ON LINE SOFTWARE INTL	MAY	NA	25.2A	28.7	36.3	63.6	81.9	NA	NA	NA	NA	NA	..	..	..	..

(cont'd)

Data by Standard & Poor's Compustat Services, Inc.

In the biographical sketch in *Who's Who in Finance and Industry* (Figure 3-6), we see that Mr. Akers, Chairman of the Board of IBM, graduated from Yale University in 1956. In 1960, after military service, he went to work for IBM and spent his entire career there. He serves on the boards of several organizations including the New York Times Company. He is a trustee of the Metropolitan Museum of Art and the California Institute of Technology.

If you don't find the person you're looking for in *Who's Who in Finance and Industry*, try *Who's Who in America* or *Standard & Poor's Register of Corporations, Directors and Executives*, Volume 2, which is a biographical directory of corporate directors and executives. Another good source is the *Reference Book of Corporate Managements*. If you'd like more than just a sketch, look them up by name or by the name of the company in *Business Periodicals Index, Business Index,* or the *Wall Street Journal, New York Times,* or *National Newspaper* indexes.

Company History

At this point you are ready to dig into the history of the company. All the sources on the following worksheet can help you, but one of the most succinct accounts of a company's history can be found quickly in *Moody's Manuals*. Moody's publishes manuals for various areas: industry, transportation, banking and finance, etc. Libraries usually keep a small index volume on the shelf with these manuals so that you can find a company quickly in the various volumes.

IBM appears in the *Industrial Manual* volumes as you see it in Figure 3-7. The corporate history tells you that the company was incorporated in New York in 1911. It then goes on to describe the nature of IBM's business in some detail.

Following the text and lists of officers and directors are financial statements. They give income statement and balance sheet data for 1987 and 1988. They also present a number of financial and operating ratios going back for several years. Other sources of corporate history are the annual report, company literature and books you may find using the library's catalog.

FIGURE 3-6.   *Who's Who In Finance and Industry.*

AKERS, JOHN FELLOWS, information processing company executive; b. Boston, Dec. 28, 1934; s. Kenneth Fellows and Mary Joan (Reed) A.; m. Susan Davis, Apr. 16, 1960; children: Scott, Pamela, Anne. B.S., Yale U., 1956. With IBM Corp., Armonk, N.Y., 1960—, v.p., asst. group exec., 1976-78, v.p., group exec., 1978-82, sr. v.p., group exec., 1982-83, pres., dir., 1983—, chief exec. officer, 1985—, chmn., 1986—; also dir.; dir. N.Y. Times Co. Mem. adv. bd. Yale Sch. Orgn. and Mgmt.; bd. dirs. Council for Fin. Aid to Edn.; trustee Met. Mus. Art, Calif. Inst. Tech., Inst. Advanced Study; bd. govs. United Way Am. Served to lt. USNR, 1956-60. Office: IBM Corp Old Orchard Rd Armonk NY 10504

FIGURE 3-7. Part of an entry from *Moody's Industrial Manual.*

MOODY'S INDUSTRIAL MANUAL 457

INTERNATIONAL BUSINESS MACHINES CORPORATION

CAPITAL STRUCTURE

LONG TERM DEBT

Issue	Rating	Amount Outstanding	Times Charges Earned 1988	1987	Interest Dates	Call Price	Price Range 1988	1987
1. Deb. 9³/₈s, 2004	Aaa	$363,000,000			A&O 1	③103.05	102¹/₂- 96⁵/₈	105¹/₄- 89⁷/₈
2. Conv. subord. deb. 7⁷/₈s, 2004	Aaa	1,254,000,000			M&N 2 1	②104.725	105³/₄- 99¹/₂	131¹/₂- 97⁵/₈
3. Notes 10¹/₄% notes, 1995	Aaa	500,000,000	14.18	18.79	A&O 1 5	④100	110¹/₈- 102	116¹/₄- 99
4. 4.9% notes, due 1998	Aaa	500,000,000			M&N 1	⑤100	101³/₈- 96³/₈	
5. Other domestic debt	. . . . .	5,226,000,000			. . . . .	. . . . .	. . . . . .	. . . . .
6. Other debt	. . . . .	2,307,000,000			. . . . .	. . . . .	. . . . . .	. . . . .

CAPITAL STOCK

Issue	Par Value	Rating	Shares Outstanding	Earned per Sh. 1988	1987	Divs. per Sh. 1988	1987	Call Price	Price Range 1988	1987
1. Common	$1.25	. . . . .	①592,444,409	①$9.27	①$8.72	$4.40	$4.40	. . . . .	129¹/₂- 104¹/₂	175⁷/₈- 100

①Based on average shs. as reported by Co. ②Beginning Nov. 1988. ③Subject to change; see text. ④Beginning Oct. 15, 1992. ⑤Beginning May 1, 1995.

HISTORY

Incorporated in New York June 16, 1911 as Computing-Tabulating-Recording Co., a consolidation of Computing Scale Co. of America Tabulating Machine Co., International Time Recording Co. of New York and Bundy Manufacturing Co.

In Nov., 1921 acquired Ticketograph Co. of Chicago. In Mar., 1922 absorbed Peirce Accounting Machine Co. On Feb. 14, 1924 merged International Business Machines Corp. and assumed the name of that company.

In May, 1931, acquired exclusive world rights to the Filene-Finlay translator, a system of multiple simultaneous translation. In Aug., 1932, acquired counting and weighing machine division of National Scale Corp. of Chicopee Falls, Mass.

addition to certain cash payments and other considerations granted to Aetna by Co. under the agreement, Aetna could receive a future payment from Co. depending on the market value of MCI's stock at the time of the merger.

In exchange for the SBS assets and operations, MCI would issue to Co. 47,000,000 shs. of its com. stock.

The agreement also calls for, under certain conditions, future cash investments by Co. of $400,000,000 in MCI's securities between Sept. 1, 1986 and Dec. 31, 1988. Co. said it would not increase its total interest in MCI's com. stock beyond 30% without MCI's approval.

In 1986, Co. entered into agreements with MCI under which IBM received approximately 47 mil.

tems, workstations, typewriters, educational and testing materials, and related supplies and services. Most products are sold or leased through IBM's worldwide marketing organizations. Selected products are marketed and distributed through authorized dealers and remarketers.

Restructuring: Co. announced a major restructuring of IBM's business to make the company still more competitive and increasingly responsive to worldwide customer requirements.

The restructuring includes:

Establishment of five new, highly independent systems and technology businesses with significant worldwide responsibilities;

Creation of a new organization: IBM United

MOODY'S INDUSTRIAL MANUAL 459

Introduction of the midrange Application System/400 family was the result of a worldwide effort combining IBM teams working closely with customers and IBM Business Partners in marketing and software development. By the time of the first shipment, more than 2,500 applications were available, along with unprecedented support, education and follow-on products. The response from both current and new customers has been extremely positive.

We added new, higher-performance models to our Personal System/2 (PS/2) family of products and delivered enhancements to Operating System/2 software that allow customers to take advantage of the PS/2's Micro Channel Architecture.

New communications products improve customers' ability to connect IBM products and those of other companies; with a higher-speed Token-Ring Network and improvements to our NetView software, IBM strengthened its leadership in network management solutions.

Our range of operating system software provides a platform for customers to plan their growth into the 1990's. Key to that growth is IBM's Systems Application Architecture (SAA), which will allow users to look at and work with applications in a consistent way across IBM's product line. In 1988, we introduced SAA-supported data base and communications software products and continued to provide customers and software developers with clear direction for their own development work.

While managing the business efficiently, we are

specialists whose resources and skills complement our own. These partners, who add nearly 50 percent to our direct sales force, are increasingly important to IBM; we rely on them to reach and support the majority of Personal System/2 and Applications System/400 customers worldwide.

Kaspar V. Cassani to Retire

In December, Kap Cassani relinquished his position as Vice Chairman of the Board in anticipation of his retirement in 1989. his career as an international business leader brought distinction to him and to the company he has served so well for 37 years, most of them in Europe. Kap made especially significant long-term contributions to IBM's international growth and success as head of Africa operations. His keen insight and wise counsel were never more valuable than in his most recent assignment in the United States, and services organizations. As he returns to Europe and prepares to retire, he has our every good wish and heartfelt thanks.

Confidence in the Future

We compete in a global marketplace, and IBM is uniquely positioned to bring worldide resources to bear on solving cutomers' specific problems and achieving their individual goals. We can call on an unmatched technology base, sustained investment and exceptional financial strength — all essential for growth in the years ahead.

Above all, we are confident because of the taelent, loyalty and energy of the people of IBM. During these very demanding times, their hard work is preparing IBM for continued leadership in

J.H. Stewart, Asst. Treas.
R.N. Mattson, Asst. Treas.
M.H. VanVranken, Asst. Contr.

Directors

(Showing Age & Principal Corporate Affiliations)

John F. Akers, (54) Chmn. and Chief Exec. Off. of IBM; Dir., The New York Times Company.

Stephen D. Bechtel, Jr., (63) Chmn., Dir. and Chief Exec. Off. of Bechtel Group, Inc., subsidiary companies; Chmn., Bechtel Investments Inc. and Sequoia Ventures, Inc.

Harold Brown, (61) Chmn., Foreign Policy Institute, The Johns Hopkins University, Washington, D.C.; and Dir., AMAX, Inc., CBS, Inc., Cummins Engine Company, Inc., Philip Morris, Inc. and Synergen, Inc..

James E. Burke, (64) Chmn. & Chief Exec. Off., Johnson & Johnson; Dir., The Prudential Insurance Co. of America, and United Negro College Fund, Inc.

Frank T. Cary, (68) Retired Chmn. of IBM; Dir., Capital Cities/ABC Inc.; DNA Plant Technology Corp.; Hospital Corp. of America, J.P. Morgan & Co., Merck & Co., New York Stock Exchange, PepsiCo, Inc., and Texaco, Inc.

William T. Coleman, Jr., (68) Partner, O'Melveny & Myers; and Dir., AMAX, Inc., Chase Manhattan Bank, Chase Manhattan Corp., Cigna Corp., Pan American World Airways, PepsiCo, Inc., and Philadelphia Electric Co.

Thomas F. Frist, Jr. (50) Chmn. & Chief Exec.

460 MOODY'S INDUSTRIAL MANUAL

INCOME ACCOUNTS (Cont'd):

	1988	1987	
Interest expense	709,000	485,000	475,00(
Earnings before income taxes	9,033,000	8,630,000	8,407,00(
Provision for income taxes	3,542,000	3,372,000	3,618,00(
Net earnings before cumulative effect of accounting change	5,491,000	5,258,000	4,789,00(
Cumulative effect of change in accounting for income taxes	315,000	. . . . . .	. . . . . .
Net earnings	5,806,000	5,258,000	4,789,00(
Retained earnings, beg. of year	27,234,000	27,834,000	29,016,00(
Cash dividends	2,609,000	2,654,000	2,698,00(
Purchase & sales of treas. stock	118,000	117,000	128,00(
Capital stock purchased & retired	1,373,000	1,305,000	899,00(
Retained earnings, end of year	31,186,000	29,016,000	27,834,00(
SUPPLEMENTARY P & L DATA			
Maintenance & repairs	2,077,000	2,152,000	2,120,00(
Taxes, other than income	①	602,000	① . . . . . .

①Amount is less than 1% of total revenue.

Consolidated Statement of Cash Flows, years ended Dec. 31 (in millions of dollars):

BALANCE SHEETS

COMPARATIVE CONSOLIDATED BALANCE SHEETS, AS OF DEC. 31

(In thousands of dollars)

ASSETS	1988	1987
Current assets:		
Cash	1,072,000	782,000
Cash equivalents	3,103,000	2,685,000
①Marketable securities	1,948,000	3,954,000
Notes & accounts receivable, net	17,086,000	15,649,000
Other accounts receivable	1,014,000	1,092,000
Inventories	9,565,000	8,659,000
Prepaid expenses & other current assets	1,555,000	1,548,000
Total current assets		
Plant, rental machines & other property	35,343,000	34,369,000
Less: Accum. depreciation	44,882,000	43,075,000
Net plant, rental machines & oth. prop.	21,456,000	20,108,000
Investments and Other Assets:	23,426,000	22,967,000

Problems And Challenges

You will also want to be aware of the company's most serious problems. You may be asked to take some part in solving them if the company hires you. *Moody's Manuals* can help there too, as can *Standard & Poor's Standard Corporation Descriptions*. Periodicals and newspapers are a good place to look to identify some problems. The 10-K report and the annual report can alert you to problems as well. The 10-K is filed each year with the Securities and Exchange Commission by companies selling stock to the public. Among other things, it reports on lawsuits in progress, changes in competitive conditions, changes in the availability of raw materials and changes in the company's level of indebtedness.

The annual report will tell you about lawsuits pending—in the notes to the financial statements. Figure 3-8 shows part of the President's letter for 1988. Note the level of the President's optimism. The tone of the letter is uniformly upbeat. There may also be warning signals about problems ahead. Earlier in the letter, Mr. Akers mentioned that 6,500 employees left IBM, and discussed the company's first restructuring in 30 years.

Try the strategy we've just used for IBM for the company you are researching, working through each of the groups of sources. Later you can take time to look for more detail in the articles and books you find. When you're finished, you should have answers to most of the questions you'd want to ask about a company before the interview.

Most of the sources will probably be fairly close together in one area of the library. If not, look them up in the library's catalog as they appear on the worksheet. If you have any trouble finding the sources, show the worksheet to the librarian. If you have any problems using any of the sources, refer to the readers' instructions in the books themselves or ask the librarians for help.

Good luck!

FIGURE 3-8.   Part of the President's letter from the 1988 *IBM Annual Report*.

New Markets and New Partners

Growth in our industry continues to create new opportunities and potential customers. One way IBM is reaching them is through alliances and joint ventures around the world, with companies including Fiat and Ericsson in Europe; Nippon Telegraph and Telephone and Mitsubishi Bank in Japan; Sears, NeXT and Supercomputer Systems, Inc., in the United States. With them, we are developing or marketing offerings that range from value-added network services, to advanced manufacturing systems, to information, shopping and banking services for the home.

During 1988, we announced an agreement with Siemens — Europe's largest electronics company — under which our ROLM Systems development and manufacturing operations will become part of Siemens Information Systems, Inc. A marketing and services company — ROLM — will be jointly owned by IBM and Siemens, and will market the products of ROLM Systems, Inc., in the United States. We expect this new arrangement will provide telecommunications customers with improved product choices and support.

To further extend market coverage, we are strengthening relationships with IBM Business Partners: agents, dealers, industry and applications specialists whose resources and skills complement our own. These partners, who add nearly 50 percent to our direct sales force, are increasingly important to IBM; we rely on them to reach and support the majority of Personal System/2 and Application System/400 customers worldwide.

Kaspar V. Cassani to Retire

In December, Kap Cassani relinquished his position as Vice Chairman of the Board in anticipation of his retirement in 1989. His career as an international business leader brought distinction to him and to the company he has served so well for 37 years, most of them in Europe. Kap made especially significant long-term contributions to IBM's international growth and success as head of our World Trade Europe/Middle East/ Africa operations. His keen insight and wise counsel were never more valuable than in his most recent assignment in the United States, where he led our worldwide marketing and services organizations. As he returns to Europe and prepares to retire, he has our every good wish and heartfelt thanks.

Confidence in the Future

We compete in a global marketplace, and IBM is uniquely positioned to bring worldwide resources to bear on solving customers' specific problems and achieving their individual goals. We can call on an unmatched technology base, sustained investment and exceptional financial strength — all essential for growth in the years ahead.

Above all, we are confident because of the talent, loyalty and energy of the people of IBM. During these very demanding times, their hard work is preparing IBM for continued leadership in our industry.

While we are changing much about IBM, we have more to do. We are determined to keep customers at the center of our business — to be the very best in the world at serving them. The actions we are taking have greatly strengthened our ability to achieve that goal.

January 31, 1989, by order of the
Board of Directors

John F. Akers
Chairman of the Board

Reprinted from the IBM Corporation's *Annual Report* for 1988 by permission from the IBM Corporation.

-WORKSHEET-

INFORMATION	WHERE TO FIND IT

-I-

Call no.

name, address, telephone no. of company headquarters; names of officers; size of corporate staff; sales, products, services	_____ Standard & Poor's Register of Corporations, Directors, and Executives
	_____ Dun & Bradstreet Million Dollar Directory
	_____ Thomas Register of American Manufacturers
divisions, subsidiaries, affiliates	_____ Directory of Corporate Affiliations
	_____ America's Corporate Families: The Billion Dollar Directory

-II-

rank of company among large corporations (with assets, net income, sales, no. employees)	_____ Fortune Directory
	_____ Forbes, "Annual Directory Issue," each April
rank of company among large corporations (with stockholders' equity, earnings per share, growth in earnings per share)	_____ Fortune Directory
	_____ Forbes, "Annual Report on American industry," each January
standing of a company in its industry or field	_____ Value Line Investment Survey
	_____ Standard & Poor's Industry Surveys

INFORMATION	WHERE TO FIND IT
	_____ Forbes, "Annual Report on American Industry," each January
	_____ Business Week, "Corporate Scoreboard," each March
	_____ Fortune Directory including rankings of the largest diversified service companies, commercial banking cos., life insurance cos., retailing cos., diversified financial cos., transportation cos., utilities

-III-

INFORMATION	WHERE TO FIND IT
biographical information about the officers	_____ Who's Who in Finance and Industry
	_____ Standard & Poor's Register of Corporations, Directors, and Executives
	_____ Reference Book of Corporate Managements
	_____ Who's Who in America
	_____ Business Index
	_____ Business Periodicals Index
	_____ Wall Street Journal Index
	_____ New York Times Index

INFORMATION	WHERE TO FIND IT
	_____ <u>National Newspaper Index</u>
	-IV-
history of the company	_____ <u>Moody's Manuals</u> (also give historical financial data)
	_____ Standard & Poor's Corporation. <u>Standard Corporation Descriptions.</u>
	_____ annual reports, 10-K reports
	_____ company published brochures
	_____ books (See library catalog under name of company)
	_____ journal articles. See <u>Business Index; Business Periodicals Index; Predicasts F&S Index United States</u>
	under the name of company
	_____ newspaper articles. See <u>New York Times</u>, <u>Wall Street Journal</u>, or <u>National Newspaper</u> indexes
	-V-
potentially critical problems	_____ annual reports, 10-K reports
	_____ <u>Moody's Manuals</u>
	_____ Standard & Poor's Corporation. <u>Standard Corporation Descriptions.</u>

INFORMATION	WHERE TO FIND IT
	_____ periodicals and newspapers
plans for new products, facilities, services, methods, mergers, acquisitions, etc.	_____ annual reports, 10-K reports
	_____ <u>Value Line Investment Survey</u>
	_____ journal and newspaper articles (See journal and newspaper indexes cited above.)

4
Researching A Small Business

Waiting until the last minute to research a small business is like deciding one morning to use the money you find in the street to buy your lunch. You may be able to find enough for a little nibble, but you can't count on getting much of substance. To find out about a small employer, you usually have to dig; digging takes time.

Before you start the hunt, consider the nature of the small business. Small ventures are usually owned by very independent people who dislike inquiries from outsiders into the details their business—particularly the contents of their financial statements. The smaller the business the more closely the financial statements reflect the personal income of the owners, and most people like to keep information about their incomes confidential.

Small businesses, especially new ones, are usually in risky positions. Their owners may find it a matter of survival to put the best possible face on their situations. If a stranger asks a small business owner how business is going, no matter how badly it's going, the owner will probably say, "Fine." After all, the owner is often the company's whole public relations department.

Unlike large, publicly traded corporations, small businesses have no reason to make information about themselves widely known. In fact, small businesses need report only to the Internal Revenue Service, the bank—if they are using bank financing—other lenders, and their creditors. Suppliers, competitors, customers, current and former employees may have varying amounts of information about the resources and activities of the small business. Of these, the IRS, the bank, and other major lenders will know more about a small business's finances than any of the others. If some kind of registration is required to operate, offices in state government, such as the office of the secretary of state, may be able to supply some information about

31

the company. Newspaper and trade journal editors can sometimes be helpful in providing information about a small business.

When you prepare for an interview with a small company, you will want to know: its formal name, address, size, potential for growth, stability, something about the nature, history, and personality of the business, and some biographical information about the owners.

Where could you be sure to find printed information about a small business? It seems very simple, but one place is the white or *Yellow Pages* of the telephone directory. Small companies, like all businesses, need clients and usually list themselves in telephone books. They may also be found in local business directories issued by chambers of commerce or private publishers. Small businesses are also listed in various kinds of specialized directories according to the type of business or professional group they represent.

Owners of small businesses are frequently written up in feature articles in local newspapers, local interest or business magazines, or trade literature. If you are fortunate enough to find an article about the company you're researching, you may gather some valuable detailed information. All of these resources are likely to be available to you in large public libraries serving local business. They may also be found in clipping files or vertical files the library maintains or you may find them yourself by using indexes to local newspapers or magazines.

Figure 4-1 is a good example of what you can find if you have time to track down articles in trade or general business magazines. This article from *Forbes* was written about two small business owners in Kennebunkport, Maine, and was cited in *Predicasts F&S Index United States* under the name of the company, Tom's of Maine. In a brief article, we learn something about the history of the business, the product, the owners' financial situation, their personal backgrounds and philosophies, their corporate values, and the company's prospects for growth.

Once you've exhausted the printed resources available in your library, try some other approaches. If you are a student, consider doing a research project. Students working on term projects for courses are usually able to interview individuals within the company, and sometimes that's the only way to get information about a very small business. Students and graduates can ask the placement officers in their schools for information about specific companies—or at least for some guidance about whom to approach for information.

Anyone about to interview can go to the company and ask the secretary to the president or the public relations department (if there is one) if they have a clipping file with articles about the company and its personnel. This is frequently a good source of information. If the company knows you are about to interview and have exhausted publicly available resources, they should be glad to help you. While you probably will get other information on site when you come for an interview, and you may also get to talk with

FIGURE 4-1.   Text of an article about a small business in *Forbes Magazine*.

The Up & Comers

Hearts, minds and market share

By Laura Jereski

THREE TIMES A DAY a passing freight train shakes the renovated railway depot outside Kennebunk, Me. that serves as headquarters for Thomas Chappell's company. But Chappell, his mind on bigger things, doesn't notice. Can his Tom's of Maine all-natural toothpaste and deodorant company survive against the marketing muscle power of Procter & Gamble, Colgate-Palmolive and Unilever?

Whatever his fate in the toothpaste game, this is just the life Tom Chappell, now 46, and his wife, Kate, hoped for back in 1968. A native of Pittsfield, Mass., Chappell graduated with a B.A. in English from Hartford's Trinity College in 1966, and got a job selling insurance for Aetna Life. But something was missing. "I grew up in a family where venturing was normal," says Chappell, "and I needed a more creative environment than a large corporation has to offer."

The Chappells moved to Kennebunk, where Tom's father, a textile manufacturer, was setting up a new business. There, with the help of several friends, Tom and Kate began developing a line including deodorants and toothpastes made from all-natural ingredients—coriander-based deodorant, for example, and toothpaste made from real spearmint. In their spare time Tom and Kate started an alternative elementary school. Three of the couple's five children attended.

By 1982 Tom's of Maine was a folksy success. It was earning a little money on annual sales of about $1.5 million, booked almost entirely in health food stores. Unfortunately, however, the company had saturated the health store market and growth in sales had slowed. If Chappell wanted to grow, he would have to expand into mass market outlets, even if that meant taking on the huge consumer products companies.

Chappell knew drug chains like CVS and Walgreen's were scouting for new products for health-conscious consumers. "But I didn't like the way the chains created their health product sections," he says. "I wanted Tom's on the shelf next to Crest and Colgate, competing as a natural alternative."

To earn that right, Chappell understood that he needed a more professional organization. To his board of directors he added Colin Blaydon, dean of Dartmouth's Amos Tuck School of Business, and John Rockwell, a senior vice president at consultant Booz, Allen & Hamilton. At their encouragement, he has brought in some professional managers, including Marketing Vice President John Eldredge, a veteran of General Mills, who knows the ways of his big competitors. This has added hefty salary costs—about $100,000 for each of Chappell's three full-time vice presidents—but the results thus far have been worth the cost.

Impressed by Chappell's serious approach to business and by his success in health food stores, the 760-outlet CVS drug chain agreed to stock Chappell's products next to big-name brands. Other chains followed. None has had reason to regret the decision. In Maine, where Tom's has been advertising the longest, its toothpaste, with just over 5% of the market, has just displaced Unilever's Aim as the number four brand. Nationally, Tom's is the top all-natural line.

Tom's of Maine's sales are now in excess of $8 million, on which the company will earn around $350,000 aftertax. Remember, however, that like many successful entrepreneurs, Chappell went into business for reasons other than money. "The business," he says firmly, "is for the pursuit of goodness." This year, for example, the company will give 7.5% of its aftertax profits to charities.

Two years ago, in the midst of rolling the Tom's of Maine brand out to stores from Boston to Washington, Chappell took a big step toward achieving another personal goal. He decided to pursue a longtime desire to go to divinity school. Chappell, a devout Episcopalian, now commutes some 200 miles to the Harvard Divinity School in Cambridge, Mass., where he spends three days a week. "Several of us were anxious," says Blaydon, the director, of Chappell's decision. "I wasn't quite sure what to expect—divine intervention perhaps?" No, but Chappell's educational pursuit has led to some interesting times around the office. Last summer's board meeting, for example, began with a discussion of Martin Buber's *I and Thou*, hosted by the noted theologian Richard Niebuhr, one of Chappell's divinity school professors.

But Chappell remains very much in this world. To convince the big chains that Tom's of Maine will be a strong brand, he has been spending heavily, relative to his size, on advertising. This year Tom's advertising budget will come to $1.25 million, about the same percentage of sales that Colgate spends, though a pittance compared with Colgate's dollar spending.

"Most specialized brands have a high cost of goods," says Chappell. "But they price competitively and don't have much money for advertising and marketing." Not so for Tom's of Maine. To fund this budget, Chappell has kept his prices to stores as much as 25% higher than mass market brands. His products can retail for 50% more than those of leading consumer products companies. A 3-

> *"I wanted Tom's on the shelf next to Crest and Colgate, competing as a natural alternative."*

ounce tube of Tom's all-natural toothpaste, for example, runs to $2.39, compared with about $1.65 for a 4.6-ounce tube of Colgate or Crest. Tom's 2.3-ounce coriander deodorant stick costs $3.19, compared with prices between $1.49 and $2.49 for 2-ounce sticks of brands like Ban or Sure. Chappell agrees that his pricing policy has "strained relations" with store managers and customers. But it seems to be paying off. With Tom's gaining share in its markets, and with advertising support growing, the chains are eager to sell the brand.

Chappell says he wants to keep rolling his brand into the hip, urban markets where potential customers are concentrated. Last month radio advertising began in the New York area, where the brand has been in Pathmark and Duane Reade for three years. Chappell plans to advertise in the *New York Times* this spring. His toothpaste already has a 1% market share in San Francisco.

If Tom's of Maine does as well in Boston, New York, Washington and San Francisco as it has in Portland, Me., Chappell says, it could become a $50 million company. And that would have its own rewards. "The business," emphasizes the divinity student, "has to be a financial success as well as a social success." ∎

people you know during the course of your visit, the information you get *ahead* of time is the information you can use in selling yourself in the interview.

It is unlikely that you will see the financial statements of a small business ahead of your interview, or even in advance of your hiring. You can deduce useful information about a specific business by using what we already know about types of businesses in general. Trade associations can be good sources of general information about various kinds of businesses. Books of financial and operating ratios can help you get an idea of the financial structures of types of small businesses.

Finally, if you have the time and a sufficient budget, you might pay a business consultant or an information broker to supply information. That approach lets you draw on their professional expertise and frees your time.

Using the worksheets at the end of the chapter should save you some time in finding out about a small employer, but by now you know you can't count on speed.

Directories

While limited in the number of facts they supply about an organization, directories can be very useful in leading you to people within a company who may be willing and able to respond to requests for further information. There are directories for an amazing array of businesses from accounting firms to travel agencies. Here is a very selective sampling of directories available in many libraries:

Field	Directory
Accounting	*Emerson's Directory of Leading U.S. Accounting Firms* *Who Audits America*
Advertising	*Standard Directory of Advertising Agencies*
Banking	*Polk's Bank Directory.* North American Edition *Rand McNally International Bankers Directory* National Council of Savings Institutions. *Directory* *Directory of American Savings and Loan Associations*
Consultants	*Consultants and Consulting Organizations Directory* *Dun's Consultant's Directory*
Franchisers	*Franchise Annual* *The Source Book of Franchise Opportunities*
Insurance	*Best's Insurance Reports: Life-Health*

Best's Insurance Reports: Property-Casualty

Investments | *Standard & Poor's Security Dealers of North America*

Market research | *Bradford's Directory of Marketing Research
    Agencies and Management Consultants in the United
    States and the World*
*The Green Book: International Directory of Marketing
    Research Houses and Services*

Media | *Broadcasting/Cable Yearbook*
Gale Directory of Publications

Public relations | *O'Dwyer's Directory of Public Relations Firms*

Real estate | *National Roster of Realtors*

Shopping centers | *Shopping Center Directory*

For finding directories in other fields of interest use:

Directories in Print
Encyclopedia of Associations
National Trade and Professional Associations of the United States

-WORKSHEET-

INFORMATION	WHERE TO FIND IT
	Call no.
name, address, telephone no. of company headquarters	_____ local telephone book, white and Yellow Pages; city directory
	_____ specialized directory (see list below)
	_____ Dun & Bradstreet Million Dollar Directory
	_____ Standard & Poor's Register of Corporations, Directors, and Executives
names of officers, size of staff, products, services	_____ specialized directory
	_____ local newspaper
	library clipping file
	public relations department of company if it has one
	letter or call to company itself
sales, financial information, stability, growth	personal interviews with officers, clients, suppliers, employees, creditors
	reports prepared by the company for borrowing purposes, etc.

INFORMATION		WHERE TO FIND IT
standing of a company in its industry or field		local newspaper
	_____	New York Times Index
	_____	Wall Street Journal Index
	_____	Predicasts F&S Index United States (corporate section)
	_____	Business Index
		personal interview with owner, competitors, clients, suppliers, employees, creditors, newspaper business editors, consultant
		Better Business Bureau
	_____	Robert Morris Associates. Annual Statement Studies or
	_____	Troy's Almanac of Business and Industrial Financial Ratios
biographical information	_____	local newspaper
		letter to secretary to the president or owner
	_____	Business Index
	_____	Predicasts F&S Index United States
		library clipping file
	_____	New York Times Index
	_____	Wall Street Journal Index

INFORMATION		WHERE TO FIND IT
		personal interviews
		local chamber of commerce (newsletters, etc.)
history of company	_____	local newspaper
		letter or call to secretary to the president or owner
		personal interviews
		reports prepared by the company for borrowing purposes
		interview with the president or owner
		library clipping file
potentially critical problems	_____	local newspaper
		personal interviews
		reports prepared by the company for borrowing purposes
		consultants familiar with the company
		local, state, federal government records (see How to Find Information About Companies or How to Find Information About Private Companies)

INFORMATION	WHERE TO FIND IT
new lines, processes, etc.	_____ local and other newspapers
	personal interviews
	reports prepared by the company for borrowing purposes, etc.

5

Researching A Private Company

Finding information about a small business can be difficult; finding information about a larger, privately held company can be equally challenging. Since one of the privileges of private ownership is not having to disclose financial statements to the public, secrecy can be a distinct competitive advantage for a larger, privately held company.

Like small businesses, privately held companies need report their financial situations only to lenders and the Internal Revenue Service. Because they do not report to the Securities and Exchange Commission, you will not find their financial statements among those of other large companies in collections of such reports commonly held in libraries. You may not even find them listed among other large corporations in directories of American businesses or similar sources. If you do not find a larger company listed in the sources suggested in Chapter 3, suspect that it is either a division or some other part of a parent corporation or that it is a privately held company.

One way to check on a company's status is to look for its name in the comprehensive index for the *Directory of Corporate Affiliations* or in one of the general corporate directories like *Standard & Poor's Register of Corporations* or Dun & Bradstreet's *Million Dollar Directory*. If the company is listed in any of these directories, the listing will note the stock exchange for the company if it is traded publicly. If you find no indication of an exchange, you can assume it is privately owned (or has been until fairly recently). If this yields no results, you'll save a lot of time if you ask a librarian for help.

For many privately held businesses, it is possible to use the library to find annual sales figures and the number of people employed. It is also possible to find feature articles about them in newspapers, trade magazines, and business journals. Finding detailed financial statements in print is next to impossible.

Private corporations recruiting at colleges and universities, however, usually make copies of their promotional literature available. This material usually provides general information about employees, facilities, and products, and some information about career paths in the company, but no information about any serious problems the company may be grappling with.

This is one of the times when knowing someone currently employed in the company with whom you can talk is extremely valuable. You can profit, however, by doing all possible research first in the library and basing your questions on information already at hand.

You may also feel free, in these instances, to ask the company for relevant information as you progress through various states of the hiring process. They should understand and admire your curiosity since they *know* you cannot find out more about them elsewhere. The point is to try first on your own and then ask for help after uncovering all the information you can.

Consider following a research strategy such as this:

Before first interview:

- review all material on file in the placement office
- review all material available in the library (using the Worksheet)

Before second interview:

- ask for other material company might supply such as an annual report

Before taking job:

- review financial statements or some other solid indication of the financial strength of the company
- consider whatever you can deduce from your own reliable personal sources and intuition about the company

Traditionally, a number of major accounting, consulting, and investment firms have been privately held companies. If we trace one of the largest investment banking firms, Goldman, Sachs & Company, through the sources listed on the worksheets below, the kinds of information one might find in the library will be quickly apparent.

Using either Dun & Bradstreet's *Million Dollar Directory* or *Standard & Poor's Register of Corporations*, we can find some facts about the company, but a better choice for more detailed information about a firm of this type would be a specialized directory like *Standard & Poor's Security Dealers of North America* (Figure 5-1). There we find three pages of information giving: the nature of their business, locations of regional and overseas offices, the names of the partners and other useful information.

FIGURE 5-1.   Part of a typical entry from *Standard & Poor's Security Dealers of North America*.

894   **NEW YORK**

New York City   New York City

New Issues, Options, Stocks, Bonds & Dealers in
  Mutual Fund Shares
Also Registered—NJ
Officer—Arthur Chow, Pres
Compliance—Julius C. Huang, V-P
Operations—Robert Loh, V-P
Investment—Kwok C. Leung, V-P
Sales—Alice Wong, V-P
Clear Thru—Q & R Clearing Corp. (0158-NSCC)
Registered Reps—20
Employer's Ident. No.—13-3267120
Employees—30
Phone—212—226-6868

**GOIN GOIN MANNETTA AVERY KIMM HYY
SPECIALISTS INC.**
  (+) (1958) 111 Broadway, Ste. 1308 (10006)
Stocks
Phone—212—587-8600

GOLD (E. & G.) CO.
  (+) 115 Broadway (10006)
(At Spear Leeds & Kellogg)
Options
Partners—Gilbert Gold, Edward Gold
Employer's Ident. No.—13-2919926

GOLDBERG (H. L.) & CO.
  (SIPC) (SIA) 20 Broad St. (10005)
(At Wagner, Stott & Co.)
Stocks & Bonds

GOLDMAN CAPITAL MANAGEMENT, INC.
  (NASD) (MSRB) (SIPC) (1985) One New
  York Plaza (10004)
Securities Broker-Dealers, Investment Banking,
  Private Placements, Mergers & Acquisitions &
  Investment Management
Also Registered—CA; FL; GA; MA
Officers—Neal I. Goldman, Pres & Secy; Thomas
  F. Flynn, Treas
Compliance—Neal I. Goldman
Administration & Operations—Jessica R. Horn
Clear Thru—Weiss, Peck & Greer (0022-NSCC)
Employer's Ident No.—13-3279572
Phone—212—908-9745

GOLDMAN, SACHS & CO.
  ■ (NASD) (*) (+) (SIA) (PSA) (N)
(NSCC) (MW) (MSRB) (P) (CB) (CBO)
(PC) (@) (SIPC) (1869) 85 Broad St. (10004)
Underwriters & Dealers in U.S. & International
  Equity & Debt Securities; Municipal Bonds,
  Mortgage & Asset-Backed Securities;
  Corporate Fixed Income Securities; U.S. &
  Euro Short & Medium Term Securities; U.S. &
  International Government Securities;
  Specializing in Investment Banking
ALSO REGISTERED—AL; AK; AZ; AR; CA;
CO; CT; DE; DC; FL; GA; HI; ID; IL; IN; IA;
KS; KY; LA; ME; MD; MA; MI; MN; MS;
MO; MT; NE; NH; NJ; NM; NC; ND; OH;
OK; OR; PA; RI; SC; SD; TN; TX; UT; VT;

NOTE--for footnotes see page 3

VA; WA; WV; WI; WY; Puerto Rico
REGIONAL OFFICES—Boston; Chicago;
  Dallas, TX; Detroit; Houston, TX; Los Angeles
  Memphis, TN; Miami, FL; Philadelphia; San
  Francisco
OVERSEAS OFFICES—Hong Kong, Hong
  Kong; Tokyo, Japan (Goldman Sachs
  International Limited); London, England;
  Zurich, Switzerland (Goldman, Sachs & Co.);
  Sydney, Australia (Goldman Sachs Limited);
  Singapore, Republic of Singapore; Paris,
  France; Toronto, Ont.
DIV. OFFICE-J. ARON & COMPANY—NYC
PARTNERS—(SIA) (CB) John L. Weinberg,
  Donald R. Gant, (+) Robert E. Mnuchin,
  George M. Ross (Philadelphia), (CBO) (PC)
  Robert E. Rubin, Eric P. Sheinberg, Stephen
  Friedman, Peter M. Sacerdote, Daniel W.
  Cook, III (Dallas), Leon G. Cooperman,
  Robert N. Downey, Lewis M. Eisenberg, Roy
  J. Zuckerberg, Geoffrey T. Boisi, Kenneth D.
  Brody, David C. Clapp, Peter R. Coneway
  (Houston), Robert M. Conway (London),
  Robert M. Freeman, David M. Silfen, Jon S.
  Corzine, Eugene V. Fife (London), Robert A.
  Friedman, Richard M. Hayden, Robert J.
  Hurst, William J. Kealy, Terence J. Mulvihill
  (Chicago), Peter G. Sachs, Howard A.
  Silverstein, Dennis A. Suskind, Howard C.
  Katz, Michael R. Armellino, Peter K. Barker
  (Los Angeles), Eric S. Dobkin, Peter M.
  Fahey, David A. George, Willard J. Overlock,
  Jr., Henry M. Paulson, Jr. (Chicago), Joseph
  H. Wender, Mark O. Winkelman, Eugene D.
  Atkinson, Richard S. Atlas (Los Angeles), (*)
  Jonathan L. Cohen, Alfred C. Eckert, III,
  John R. Farmer (San Francisco), (SIA) Robe
  C. Frahm, II, Fredric B. Garonzik, J.
  Markham Green, Kevin W. Kennedy, Joel
  Kirschbaum, William C. Landreth (London),
  Gordon McMahon, Daniel M. Neidich, Gary
  D. Rose, Edward Spiegel, Victor R. Wright
  (London), Thomas W. Berry, Fischer Black,
  Robert A. Cenci, Robert F. Cummings, Jr.,
  Charles A. Davis, Angelo De Caro (London),
  Michael C. Delaney, David F. DeLucia, Steve
  G. Einhorn, Joseph H. Ellis, Wade Fetzer, II
  (Chicago), David B. Ford, Robert M. Giordan
  John A. Golden, Richard W. Herbst, Paul F.
  Jacobson, P. Henry James, James N. Lane,
  David M. Leuschen, Jeanette W. Loeb,
  Michael R. Lynch, Michael D. McCarthy,
  Thomas G. Mendell, Todd M. Morgan, Robe
  E. O'Hara III, Donald C. Opatrny, Jr., John
  J. Oros, R. Ralph Parks, Jr., Edward A.
  Poppiti, Jr., Thomas R. Pura, Thomas L.
  Rhodes, Jacob Z. Schuster, Gary L. Seevers,
  Alan A. Shuch, Thomas E. Tuft, Artur Walth
  Garland E. Wood, George F. Adam, Jr.,
  Michael P. Mortara, Henry C. Barkhorn, II
  Lloyd Blankfein, Frank P. Brosens, John P.

If we consulted *Forbes'* list of "Largest Private Companies in the U.S.," we would find that Goldman, Sachs ranks 31 out of the 400 largest private companies. If we looked at *Ward's* directory, we could find a list of the names and annual sales of its competitors—both public and private investment firms (Figure 5-2).

Biographical sketches of John L. Weinberg, Goldman, Sachs & Company's senior partner, appear in the major biographical directories on the worksheet. If we look at the one in *Who's Who in America* (Figure 5-3), we can find out about his family, his education, his career with Goldman, Sachs, his military experience, the boards he serves on, and his various other memberships. A recent article in *Forbes* for September 18, 1989, also gives some fascinating information about Mr. Weinberg and the future of Goldman, Sachs—raising questions about whether it will remain a private com-

---

FIGURE 5-2.   From *Ward's Business Directory of U.S. Private and Public Companies.*

6211 Security Brokers & Dealers

1 Shearson Lehman Hutton Holding Inc.	American Express Tower	New York	NY	10285	212-298-2000	P	10,529	40.9
2 Salomon Bros. Inc.	1 New York Plaza	New York	NY	10004	212-747-7000	S	5,256	6.2
3 Drexel Burnham Lambert Inc.	60 Broad St.	New York	NY	10004	212-232-6000	R	4,400	9.0
4 Merrill Lynch, Pierce, Fenner & Smith Inc.	World Financial North T	New York	NY	10281	212-449-1000	S	2,904	35.7
5 PaineWebber Inc.	1285 Ave. of the Americ	New York	NY	10019	212-713-2000	S	2,512	N/A
6 Dean Witter Financial Services Inc.	2 World Trade Center	New York	NY	10048	212-392-2222	S	2,480	N/A
7 Goldman Sachs & Co.	85 Broad St.	New York	NY	10004	212-902-1000	R	2,402	6.1
8 Morgan Stanley & Co. Inc.	1251 Ave. of the Americ	New York	NY	10020	212-703-4000	S	1,353	5.0
9 Prudential-Bache Securities Inc.	199 Water St.	New York	NY	10292	212-776-1000	S	1,230*	17.0
10 Massachusetts Investors Trust (Boston, MA)	P.O. Box 2281	Boston	MA	02107	617-954-5000	R	1,177	N/A
11 E.F. Hutton & Co. Inc.	31 W. 52nd St.	New York	NY	10019	212-298-2000	S	1,114	16.5
Shearson Lehman Hutton Holding Inc.								
12 Smith Barney, Harris Upham & Co. Inc.	1345 Ave. of the Americ	New York	NY	10105	212-399-6000	S	1,005	6.1
13 Donaldson, Lufkin & Jenrette Securities Corp.	140 Broadway	New York	NY	10005	212-504-3000	S	800*	3.3
14 Kidder, Peabody & Co. Inc.	10 Hanover Sq.	New York	NY	10005	212-510-3000	S	676	7.2
15 United Investors Management Co.	2001 Third Ave. S.	Birmingham	AL	35233	205-325-4200	P	639	1.1
16 Oppenheimer & Co. Inc.	Oppenheimer Tower	New York	NY	10281	212-667-7000	R	560	2.3
17 Charles Schwab Corp.	101 Montgomery St.	San Francisco	CA	94104	415-627-7000	P	392	2.1
18 Allen & Co.	711 5th Ave.	New York	NY	10022	212-832-8000	R	377	< .1
19 Thomson McKinnon Securities Inc.	Financial Sq.	New York	NY	10005	212-804-8674	S	305	5.0
20 Nikko Securities Co. Intl. Inc.	200 Liberty St., Tower	New York	NY	10281	212-416-5400	S	263	.3
21 Aubrey G. Lanston & Co.	20 Broad St.	New York	NY	10005	212-943-1200	S	244	.1
22 A.G. Edwards & Sons Inc.	1 N. Jefferson Ave.	St. Louis	MO	63103	314-289-3000	S	243	6.4
23 Van Kempen Merritt	1001 Warrenville Rd.	Lisle	IL	60532	708-719-6000	S	241	.5
24 Spear Leeds & Kellogg	115 Broadway	New York	NY	10006	212-587-8800	R	238	.9
25 Dillon, Read & Co. Inc.	535 Madison Ave.	New York	NY	10022	212-906-7000	S	224	.7
26 Nomura Securities Intl. Inc.	180 Maiden Ln.	New York	NY	10038	212-208-9300	S	223	.6

Reprinted from *Ward's Business Directory of U.S. Private and Public Companies*, 1990 ed., by permission of Gale Research, Inc.

FIGURE 5-3.   *Who's Who in America.*

WEINBERG, JOHN LIVINGSTON, investment banker; b. N.Y.C., Jan. 5, 1925; s. Sidney James and Helen (Livingston) W.; m. Sue Ann Gotshal, Dec. 6, 1952; children: Ann K. (dec.), John, Jean. A.B. cum laude, Princeton U., 1948; M.B.A., Harvard U., 1950. With Goldman, Sachs & Co., N.Y.C., 1950—, partner, 1956-76, sr. ptnr., 1976—, co-chmn. mgmt. com., 1976-84, chmn. mgmt. com., 1984—; bd. dirs. B.F. Goodrich Co., Kraft, Inc., Knight-Ridder, Inc., Seagram Co. Ltd., Capital Holding Corp., E.I. du Pont de Nemours & Co.; mem. Conf. Bd., N.Y.C. Ptnrship., Inc. Bd. govs., mem. exec. com. N.Y. Hosp.; mem. adv. Council Stanford U. Bus. Sch.; charter trustee Princeton U. Served to 2d lt. USMCR, 1942-46; capt. 1951-52. Mem. Chgo. Bd. Trade, Council on Fgn. Relations, Japan Soc. (bd. dirs.). Clubs: Economic (N.Y.C.); Blind Brook, Century Country. Office: Goldman Sachs & Co 85 Broad St New York NY 10004

Copyright © 1988-89, Marquis Who's Who, Inc. Reprinted by permission from *Who's Who In America*, 1988-89, 45th edition.

pany, its relationship with a major Japanese institutional partner, and its changing corporate culture.

Directories

Directories can be useful in leading you to people within a company who may respond to requests for further information. An amazing array of businesses, from accounting firms to travel agencies, are included in a wide variety of directories. Here is a very selective sampling of directories available in many libraries.

Field	Directory
Accounting	*Emerson's Directory of Leading U.S. Accounting Firms* *Who Audits America*
Advertising	*Standard Directory of Advertising Agencies*
Banking	*Polk's Bank Directory*. North American Edition *Rand McNally International Bankers Directory* National Council of Savings Institutions. *Directory* *Directory of American Savings and Loan Associations*
Consultants	*Consultants and Consulting Organizations Directory* *Dun's Consultant's Directory*
Franchisers	*Franchise Annual* *The Source Book of Franchise Opportunities*
Insurance	*Best's Insurance Reports: Life-Health* *Best's Insurance Reports: Property-Casualty*
Investments	*Standard & Poor's Security Dealers of North America*
Market research	*Bradford's Directory of Marketing Research Agencies and Management Consultants in the United States and the World* *The Green Book: International Directory of Marketing Research Houses and Services*
Media	*Broadcasting/Cable Yearbook* *Gale Directory of Publications*
Public relations	*O'Dwyer's Directory of Public Relations Firms*

Real estate   *National Roster of Realtors*

Shopping centers   *Shopping Center Directory*

For finding directories in other fields of interest use:

Directories in Print
Encyclopedia of Associations
National Trade and Professional Associations of the United States

-WORKSHEET-

INFORMATION		WHERE TO FIND IT
		-I-
		Call no.
name, address, telephone no. of company headquarters; names of officers; size of corporate staff; sales, products, services	_____	Standard & Poor's Register of Corporations, Directors, and Executives
	_____	Dun & Bradstreet Million Dollar Directory
	_____	Thomas Register of American Manufacturers
	_____	Ward's Business Directory of U.S. Private and Public Companies
divisions, subsidiaries, affiliates	_____	Directory of Corporate Affiliations
	_____	America's Corporate Families The Billion Dollar Directory
		-II-
rank of company	_____	"INC's 500 Fastest Growing Privately Owned Smaller Corporations" INC (December issue)
	_____	"Largest Private Companies in the U.S." Forbes (November or December issue)
standing of a company in its industry or field	_____	Ward's Business Directory of U.S. Private and Public Companies

INFORMATION	WHERE TO FIND IT

-III-

biographical information about the officers	_____ Who's Who in Finance and Industry
	_____ Standard & Poor's Register of Corporations, Directors, and Executives
	_____ Reference Book of Corporate Managements
	_____ Who's Who in America
	_____ Business Index
	_____ Business Periodicals Index
	_____ Wall Street Journal Index
	_____ New York Times Index
	_____ National Newspaper Index

-IV-

history of the company	_____ company published brochures
	_____ books (See library catalog under name of company)
	_____ journal articles. See Business Index; Business Periodicals Index; Predicasts F&S Index United States under the name of company
	_____ newspaper articles. See New York Times, Wall Street Journal, or National Newspaper indexes, and local and regional newspapers

INFORMATION	WHERE TO FIND IT
	-V-
potentially critical problems	periodicals and newspapers
	personal interviews
	reports prepared by the company for borrowing purposes
	consultants familiar with the company
———————	local, state, federal government records (See How to Find Information About Companies or How to Find Information About Private Companies)
plans for new products, facilities, services, methods, mergers, acquisitions, etc.	journal and newspaper articles (See journal and newspaper indexes cited above.)
	personal interviews
	reports prepared by the company for borrowing purposes
	consultants familiar with the company

6
Elegant, Information Age Research

This is the age of the knowledge worker, the desktop computer, and a whole industry devoted to the collection and dissemination of information. How can you take advantage of new technology to find out about your best employer?

Until now we have considered using standard publications found in almost any business collection. If you have the inclination and the financial resources to take advantage of services described in this chapter, you will be able to save time and effort. Using electronic databases eliminates searching for specific books and journals, which your library many not even have, and may even provide some of the basic business analysis we've been talking about. You'll be able to gain access to timely reports written by financial analysts, market researchers, and consultants, and you'll be able to locate information unavailable elsewhere.

There is one big consideration in all this: You may have to pay. For years many of us have thought of information as being free—probably because public libraries are often called "free." It never has been. Philanthropists, taxpayers, tuition, and corporate gifts have funded our access to information. Today's information age technologies make gathering, storing, and high speed transmission of great masses of information possible. The additional cost of this technology is significant, readily identifiable, and therefore more likely to be billed to you. In deciding whether to use some of the products of the information age, you will want to consider that the more information you receive, and the more the information has been manipulated in some way—either by an information broker, a database vendor, or a business analyst, the more you will have to pay for it.

You may not want to make this additional investment. Some people prefer to do their own manual searching in indexes. Depending on the topic, their results can be just as good as they would be searching by computer. For many consumers, however, computerized online bibliographic searching, searching with compact disk-read only memory (CD-ROM) technology, fee-based information services, document delivery services, full-text transmission online, and purchase of expert corporate analyses are convenient, time-saving approaches well worth the costs involved.

The purpose of this chapter is to give you some idea of what the possibilities are. Because considerable expense can be involved occasionally, you need to consult with your librarian or another information professional to choose a method that will give you the best possible return on your investment.

Where can you find this help? A large public library, your own academic library, and your own corporate library are the best places to begin. Librarians in any of these kinds of libraries may either provide these services to you or direct you to fee-based services available locally or at a distance.

If you find computerized online searching in your area, either through the library or an information broker, how do you procede? Usually, you and the librarian discuss your objective. If it is just to find out about a specific company, the search strategy will be very simple. Among other things, you may specify that you want only material written in the last few years, or that you want to know about some specific aspect of the company. If you know something about the databases described later in this chapter, you'll be able to help the librarian choose the best ones to search.

For example, suppose you're just having a hard time finding out anything about a given company—even where it is. By using databases giving directory information for a large number of companies of varying sizes, you will have a good chance of at least getting the address and telephone number so that you can call or write the company for more information. You may also be able to get some of the company's financial data online.

In addition to directory and financial information, an online search can help you find detailed discussions of specific aspects of a company's situation in journal articles. That's particularly helpful if you are interested in a large company about which a great deal is written, and you don't have time to sift through all of it, or if you're interested in a small company you'd have to search a long time to find.

For example, finding a new, small business called Chez Croissant somewhere in California could be difficult and time consuming, but an online search of *Trade and Industry Index* (Figure 6-1) gave us a citation to an article about Chez Croissant that appeared in the *San Jose Business Journal* in July, 1985 (Figure 6-2). Once we got online, the whole search took less than one minute. If you live in the San Jose area, you could find the newspaper in a local library or hire an information broker to get it for you. If you must send away for an article, your librarian could tell you the best way to get it—possibly through the library's interlibrary loan program or by fax transmission. Once you and the librarian have agreed on a search strategy and

FIGURE 6-1.   Results of an online search of *Trade & Industry Index*, January 8, 1990.

```
          b148

                   08jan90 10:43:06

           File 148:TRADE AND INDUSTRY INDEX 81-90/JAN
                      (COPR. 1990 IAC)
           *************************************** **
           Trade & Industry Index is now updated  ** **
           every week.                            ** **
           ** **  For more current information from this  **
           **     database, see Newsearch, File 211.      **
           *********************************************



           Set   Items   Description
           ---   -----   -----------
?ss chez()croissant

           S1     67   CHEZ
           S2     25   CROISSANT
           S3      1   CHEZ()CROISSANT



 3/5/1
 03865244   DIALOG File 148: TRADE & INDUSTRY INDEX
Four Vietnamese women bake their way to success with croissants.
 Koland, Cordell
 Business Journal-San Jose p10(1) July 22, 1985
 SOURCE FILE: TI File 148   SUBFILE: ABD
 ARTICLE TYPE: biography
 GEOGRAPHIC CODE: NNUSWCAJ
 GEOGRAPHIC LOCATION: San Jose, California
 SIC CODE: 2051; 5149; 5462
 BIOGRAPHEE: Nguyen, Amy
 COMPANY NAME(S): Chez Croissant Inc.
 DESCRIPTORS:   women-owned   business  enterprises---California;
 rity
     minority business enterprises---California; bakers and bakeries
     ---California

?logoff
```

chosen appropriate databases, the librarian should be able to give you a rough estimate of what the search will cost.

When the search is completed, you will have a printout citing references to journals, giving financial data or, in a number of cases, full-texts of articles

---

FIGURE 6-2.   Article reprinted from the *San Jose Business Journal*, July 22, 1985.

Four Vietnamese women bake their way to success with croissants

By CORDELL KOLAND

In a version of the American dream come true, four Vietnamese women have opened their third croissant shop in downtown San Jose, part of a growth plan that may include franchising.

The newest shop on East San Carlos Street joins existing locations on N. First Street, one near Santa Clara Street and another adjacent to San Jose City Hall, said 37-year-old Amy Nguyen, manager of Chez Croissant Inc.

Amy's sisters, Beverley Nguyen and Tammy Vu, and cousin Yvonne Nguyen do the baking.

Once the shop on San Carlos Street is successfully operating, the company plans

to open a fourth restaurant in Cupertino, Nguyen said.

Chez Croissant has been approached by four or five people who are interested in establishing franchises, Amy Nguyen said. Although she's made no definite plans on franchising, she says she's looking seriously at the possibility.

Nguyen expects the two-and-one-half-year-old Chez Croissant to exceed $1 million in annual revenue with the opening of the third restaurant. Gross profit for the two existing stores is about $200,000 annually, she said.

Nguyen attributes the success of Chez Croissant to a commitment to quality ingredients.

"Everything's fresh here—no preservatives." Avoiding canned or frozen fruit and vegetables, the owners personally shop for fresh produce every day. The company uses fresh cream and top-grade butter, Nguyen said.

Nguyen encountered a difficult road to success.

In South Vietnam in 1975, just before the fall of the South Vietnamese government, Nguyen was working for the accounting section of a U.S. air base, she said.

As fears mounted, the family, including Nguyen, her sons, two sisters and a cousin, left their homeland three days before the government fell. The last-minute efforts of an American executive saved the family, Nguyen said.

Originally locating in Sacramento with a sponsor, the family eventually moved to San Jose, adapting to a new language and culture as well as looking for employment.

The family decided to go into the baking business based on well-established skills. In Vietnam, a French baker had taught three of the women how to bake croissants. The process is a closely guarded company secret. Nguyen won't name the chef, who now lives in France.

Nguyen's newest downtown San Jose restaurant turning out these delicacies shares a city-owned building with a parking garage and Camera 3, a movie theater.

The interior is simple. Large windows dominate the space. The decor reflects a simple blue-and-white color scheme. White wrought-iron tables and chairs sit in an outdoor street-side alcove.

The restaurants cater to the breakfast and lunch trade as well as the take-out business.

The principal bakery is located at 1090 N. First Street. Here, the company prepares daily the croissant dough that is delivered to the other restaurants for final baking—fresh-baked croissants are the backbone of the business, Nguyen said.

Bread and French pastry are also prepared at this site near City Hall. From this location, Chez Croissant delivers fresh-baked products to corporate clients such as the Hyatt, Hilton and LeBaron hotels.

Nguyen is surprised by the young company's growth. "When I started three years ago, I didn't imagine that our product would be so well received by the customers—that today we would have three stores in three years."

By permission of the *San Jose Business Journal*.

online. You can see citations for articles you'd like to read, and most bibliographic databases can print abstracts or summaries of the articles so you can immediately get a good idea of their usefulness. You can then either find the journals in your own library, or your librarian can help you locate them elsewhere.

If you don't have a database searching service in your library, ask your reference librarian for suggestions about where to find one. Many reference departments keep a file of information brokers who do online searching for a fee. Or you can use the directories suggested below to find these services for yourself.

What are information brokers? They are librarians and information specialists who have gone into business for themselves as database searchers. Organizing information, indexing it, delivering documents, and monitoring corporations and industries have become increasingly marketable services. The flexibility and responsiveness of these small to medium-size firms have made them very useful to companies and individuals for special projects, confidential assignments, and getting access to information in a timely way. If you call on information brokers for help, you need to remember that you'll be engaging the services of professionals, and you'll pay not only for the searches or documents delivered but also for their time.

All information brokers are willing to discuss fees before undertaking any work though some of them have minimum fees. Most of them will give you an estimate before they start their work. Many information brokers do corporate and industry searches, but the directories listed later in this chapter will help you get specific information about their subject specialities. A personal reference, or "word of mouth," is one of the best ways to find information brokers, but you will also find them listed in the *Yellow Pages* of your telephone book under "Information Bureaus," or "Research Services."

Most online searching is done by professional librarians with special training, but you can perform computerized database searches yourself. While it takes some time and effort to learn to do even simple searches, and errors while you're learning can be costly, you may find it worthwhile if you already have the computer hardware and will need to do a number of searches. If you only want a search to find out about a company before an interview, investing in the equipment and getting set up to do online searches for yourself would be grossly impractical. In case you are interested in investigating the possibilities for searching online for yourself, the names of vendors can be found below.

An easier way to use modern technology to perform a literature search yourself is to use CD-ROM readers. Five systems now fairly widely available are particularly useful for getting business information. They are *ABI/Inform Ondisc, InfoTrac,* Lotus' *CD/Corporate, Compact Disclosure,* and *Business Periodicals Index.* All five systems can be searched with little or no training.

Because the expense of setting up a CD-ROM system can be considerable, you may not find all of these systems in your library. When you do find them, however, you probably won't have to pay to search them. Most of a library's expenses are incurred when a CD-ROM system is installed, so billing back each search to a user is a problem. Online searching, in contrast, is readily billable search by search because precise records of costs are created by the vendor each time a user logs onto the telephone network.

ABI/Inform Ondisc and *InfoTrac* are the easiest of these systems to use and are particularly helpful when you need speedy access to recent information on a company. With *Compact Disclosure* on CD-ROM you will be able to find the same kind of material available in *Disclosure* online (see description below). *CD/Corporate* gives access to a wide variety of information on companies, industries, kinds of business and corporate executives including: company profiles, recent and historical financial data, industry information, citations to journal articles, stock reports and investment reports prepared by securities analysts from leading investment banks and financial research organizations. *Business Periodicals Index* on CD-ROM will give you the same citations you could find in the printed version but much more quickly. The advantage in using these systems is that they are extremely user-friendly, usable at your own pace, and most likely at no charge to you. The information available on CD-ROM necessarily lags somewhat behind information from interactive database searching which can be current up to the minute.

Suppose you'd just like to skip a few steps and have someone else prepare an analytical report for you on the company you're interested in. You might use an online search to find citations to reports from brokerage houses, consulting firms, or market research companies. Your librarian will know which databases can be used for this purpose. Once you've identified a study of interest online, you can order the report from the publisher—a process that sometimes can be handled online as well. While some of these reports are available for modest cost, some can cost up to thousands of dollars.

"Caveat emptor" is still a good maxim for the information age, but "Buyer be aware" seems equally appropriate. Keep them both in mind as you look over these databases and directories which can help you do elegant, information age research. Following is a list of useful resources for finding out about a company.

I. Databases on CD-ROM

ABI/Inform Ondisc: Provides indexing to over 800 business periodicals of managerial and executive interest. It includes bibliographic information and abstracts of articles about corporations, industries, and various functional areas of business. The database corresponds to *ABI/Inform* online, long considered to be one of the best of all the management databases.

Business Periodicals Index: Indexes 345 English-language business magazines. Especially good for finding articles about major corporations and a wide range of business subjects such as advertising, computers, international business, small business, personnel administration and many others.

CD/Corporate: An amalgam of databases in one giant collection, *CD/Corporate* gives the user speedy access to a mass of information about more than 12,000 publicly traded U.S. corporations. It includes seven years of historical financial statements, excerpts from annual reports, more than 9,000 executive biographies, 11 years of stock prices, and abstracts from more than 1,000 business and trade periodicals.

Compact Disclosure: Gives access to extracts of 10-K, 10-Q, 8-K, and 20-F reports, proxy statements, management discussions and registration reports filed with the SEC by 12,800 companies listed on the New York, American, and Over-the-Counter stock exchanges.

InfoTrac: Its *General Periodicals Index* gives access to 900 periodicals and newspapers at least 675 of which are business publications. InfoTrac covers a number of local and regional business publications and is more helpful than the other CD-ROM systems for finding articles about smaller businesses and private companies.

II. Online Databases

Note: All the databases listed here are available on the two most popular online searching systems, Dialog and BRS. When you talk with the person who will do your search, check on the availability of others. Some of the most useful databases are available by other subscriptions. They are described in various guides to online databases but are not included in this outline.

Databases Providing Directory Information About U.S. Companies

These online databases will give you directory information for all the companies they cover. The particular advantage in using them is that you may be able to find small to medium-size companies not listed in standard sources. With addresses and telephone numbers, you can call for information not available in published sources.

D&B—Dun's Market Identifiers: Includes address, product, marketing and financial information for more than 2,300,000 companies, public and private, having 5 or more employees or $1,000,000 or more in sales.

D&B—Million Dollar Directory: Covers 160,000 publicly and privately owned companies with a net worth of $500,000 or more. Corresponds to Dun & Bradstreet's printed *Million Dollar Directory*.

D&B—Dun's Electronic Yellow Pages: Gives directory information for about 8.2 million U.S. businesses and professionals. Provides addresses, telephone numbers, business descriptions, and employee size range. Includes listings for such industries as construction, finance, manufacturing, retailing, services, and wholesale.

Standard & Poor's Register—Corporate: Gives information for 45,000 public and private companies usually with sales over $1 million. Its printed counterpart is Volume 1 of *Standard and Poor's Register of Corporations, Directors, and Executives*.

Trinet U.S. Businesses: Covers a wide variety of public and private businesses. Particularly good for finding privately held businesses, it includes information about market share and top executives. The database covers individual locations; aggregate company information can be found on its companion file, *Trinet Company Database*.

Databases Providing Financial Information About U.S. Companies

Disclosure Database: Gives extracts of 10-K, 10-Q and 20-F reports, and registration reports filed with the U.S. Securities and Exchange Commission by more than 12,500 companies listed on the New York, American and Over-the-Counter Stock Exchanges.

D&B— Dun's Market Identifiers: See description on page 56.

Moody's Corporate Profiles: Five-year financial histories are given for all companies on the New York and American Stock Exchanges plus about 1,800 over-the-counter companies. Data from corporate reports, news releases, proxy statements, prospectuses, etc. also included.

Moody's Corporate News—U.S.:   Gives both full text and tabular current information on about 13,000 publicly owned companies including: banks, savings and loans, insurance companies, industrials, transportation, etc. Information comes, in part, from annual reports, quarterly reports, prospectuses and proxy statements.

PTS Annual Reports Abstracts: Gives statistical abstracts of the annual reports of more than 3,000 publicly held American companies.

Trinet U.S. Businesses   See description on page 56.

Databases Covering Articles About Companies

ABI/Inform: A search of this database could be useful for finding information about the management of a particular company. Citations and abstracts of articles from more than 800 business publications are available on this popular business resource.

Area Business Databank: Can be searched online through two other databases *Trade & Industry Index* or *Newsearch*. Gives access to articles from business journals of local, state, or regional interest.

Management Contents: Includes articles from more than 120 journals, plus proceedings, transactions, research reports, newsletters that give information about various areas of general management. One can single out specific companies as they are discussed in relation to various areas of management: accounting, finance, marketing, organizational behavior, etc.

National Newspaper Index: Because this database indexes *The New York Times*, *The Wall Street Journal*, and *The Christian Science Monitor*, from front to back, and *The Los Angeles Times*, and *The Washington Post* selectively, it can be useful not only for news about business but also about other employers mentioned in articles, news reports, editorials, etc. Updated monthly, it gives timely and easy access to current information. (It does not give stock market tables.)

PAIS International: Public Affairs Information Service indexes books, journal articles, pamphlets, reports of public and private organizations, and government documents in all fields of social science. If a company has become involved in some public policy issue, information on that situation will probably be accessible through this database.

PTS F&S Index: This is a particularly useful database for corporate information including: mergers and acquisitions, new products, summaries of analyses by securities companies, and special influences on future sales and earnings.

PTS Promt: Concentrating on markets and technology, this database abstracts articles from business magazines, newspapers, trade journals, government reports, etc. Industries covered are: chemicals, communications, computers, electronics, energy, fibers, food, instruments and equipment, metals, paper, plastics and rubber. Promt gives information on acquisitions, market data, new products, regulations, environment, etc. Articles on specific companies within these industries can be singled out.

Trade & Industry Index: Indexes and selectively abstracts articles about companies found in business and trade journals, the *Wall Street Journal*, *New York Times Financial Section*, *American Banker*, *Barron's*, and the *Area Business Databank*.

Databases Giving Access to Research Reports

Arthur D. Little/Online: Gives either a bibliographic citation or full text for nonexclusive publications of Arthur D. Little, Inc. Among the industries it covers are: health care services, chemicals, energy, telecommunications, electronics, and biotechnology.

Findex Reports and Studies: This database contains over 11,500 bibliographic citations with abstracts to market research reports, studies, and surveys on many industries. It makes available company and industry reports from investment firms and major multi-client industry studies and consumer and product studies and gives ordering information for each report.

Industry Data Sources: Gives bibliographical information and abstracts for over 100,000 sources of data on 65 industries. These sources include market research reports, investment studies, working papers, and statistical reports. Information for ordering the report from the publisher is also included.

InvesText: Over 200,000 full-text research reports from leading investment banking firms are available online. Covers 8,000 publicly owned large U.S. corporations and smaller growth companies.

Directories of Databases

Any of these directories should be helpful to you for finding databases you might want to have searched or search yourself. *The Directory of Online Databases* is probably the most useful one because it is updated quarterly, and this group of services is growing and changing so quickly.

- *Computer-Readable Databases: A Directory and Data Sourcebook*
- *Data Base Directory*
- *Datapro Directory of On-Line Services*
- *Directory of Online Databases*

Database Systems You Can Search Without Extensive Training

Here are two systems you might want to investigate for yourself:

BRS After Dark: Available from:

BRS Information Technologies
A Division of Maxwell Online, Inc.
800 Westpark Drive
McLean, VA 22102
Telephone: 703/442-0900 or 800/289-4277

Knowledge Index or Dialog Business Connection: Available from:

Dialog Information Services, Inc.
3460 Hillview Avenue
Palo Alto, CA 94304
Telephone: 415/858-3810 or 800/334-2564

Directories Listing Information Brokers and Document Delivery Services:

- *Directory of Fee-Based Information Services*
- *Encyclopedia of Information Systems and Services*
- *The North American Online Directory*
- *Online Database Search Services Directory*
- *Document Retrieval Sources and Services*

7

Finding Out About Nonprofits

Not-for-profit organizations vary so much in size, objectives, and ways of operating that generalizing about them is like generalizing about business—nearly impossible. There is one fact about not-for-profits that has great bearing on finding information about them: they exist to perform a service to their publics but not to earn a profit. Therefore there are no investors to interest with reports on profitability or customers to attract with national advertising campaigns. There are, however, donors and clients to attract, members to inform, and activities to publicize. The larger the not-for-profit and the more widespread its constituency, the more available information will be.

What this means to you is that, generally speaking, not-for-profits will be harder to research than publicly owned businesses. This is particularly unfortunate because of all workers, not-for-profit people have to believe in the organization's cause. Finding out what the cause is and how effectively it is being served will be very important to you in finding your best employer.

Because they know their names are not exactly household words, many not-for-profits will not expect you to know very much about them before your interview—unless you're interviewing for a top or middle management job. People who are being considered for those positions usually know their organizations quite well already. Executive directors of professional associations, administrators of universities, and various kinds of religious leaders often come from the professional ranks of their organizations. People interviewing for middle management and staff positions may also be familiar with the not-for-profit, but they can probably benefit most from research.

The publications listed on the following pages will give you basic information about a wide range of not-for-profits. Once you have used the library to get as much information as possible and talked with others who are personally familiar with the organization, consider another avenue of approach. Ask the public relations staff, the assistant to the director, or the director's secretary to help you with your search for information by giving you access to their files of newsletters and annual reports, journals, clippings, or other documents that might be useful to you in preparing for your interview. Doing this should enable you to carry out as thorough a study as possible and should also be an indication to the employer that you are an energetic, resourceful person who is taking seriously your opportunity to interview with them.

What are some of the things you'd want to know about any not-for-profit before you took a job there? Here are some suggestions:

- name, address, telephone number
- history and purpose of the organization
- biographical information about the leaders of the organization, their careers, etc.
- source of funding
- governance of the organization
- locations of operations
- size of the budget
- size of the staff
- problems the organization must deal with
- outlook for the organization, likelihood of growth
- career paths within the organization

The answers for several of these, of course, may have to wait until the interview, but having as many facts as possible beforehand can help you present yourself and maximize everyone's time during the interview.

On the worksheets that follow are outlines of publications in various subject areas. If you don't find your area of interest there, the suggestions in Chapter 11 can help you get started with your research. One of the most useful resources for finding out about a large number of not-for-profits is the *Encyclopedia of Associations*. It provides descriptions like the one for the American Cancer Society (Figure 7-1) for thousands of professional, trade, and other not-for-profit associations in the United States. Very readily you can find the association's name, address, telephone number, the titles of its publications, and the name and title of the person in charge.

Remember that almost any field of endeavor has a trade or professional organization associated with it. In most cases, these organizations provide information to potential members and members of the general public. They can make available printed materials, refer you to individuals in your vicinity who are active in their fields, and give you other advice about careers in their areas of work.

FIGURE 7-1. Selection from the *Encyclopedia of Associations*.

Section 8 — HEALTH AND MEDICAL ORGANIZATIONS ★11810★

exhibits) - 1990 Nov. 11-16, New Delhi, India. Also con-
ˉngs.

ᴸ BURN INFORMATION EXCHANGE (Burns) (NBIE)
ᵢCenter
ᴰr., Rm. 1B401   Phone: (313) 936-9666
                                       Jai K. Prasad, M.D., Co-Dir.
ᵉrs: 137. Data registry of physicians specializing in
ᶜtives are to: establish standards of burn patient care
ᵢn standards;ˉ provide etiologic information to prevent
ᵥve patient care by exchanging information on successful
ᵤrn centers, units, and programs; develop expertise of
ᶜCollects and analyzes uniform patient data on burn
ᵒlogy, mortality, morbidity, acute treatment, recons-
ᵥerates data base and maintains file on over 100,000
ᵤand statistical analyses. Researches: the role of flam-
ᵉvere burns; the effect of institutional differences on
ᵐᵗ the effectiveness of various topical agents; the gen-
ᵛal curves.

ᵉr, periodic. ● *Report*, annual.

annual - in conjunction with American Burn Associa-

ᴬᴸ BURN VICTIM FOUNDATION (Burns) (NBVF)
                                       Phone: (201) 731-3112
                                       Harry J. Gaynor, Pres.
ᴶ Members: 26. Staff: 10. Budget: $800,000. Sup-
ᵧ specializing in burn treatment and care, fire services
ᵧ nurses, communications experts, health and chemical
ᵢives, and others interested in burn treatment and care.
ᵉrgency burn referral service and crisis intervention
that provide counseling for burn victims and their fam-
ᵢⁱological problems and physical handicaps remaining after
ᵧ free blood services to burn victims. Sponsors Burns
ᵧ roup. Conducts medical emergency burn care seminars
ᵧsicians, nurses, EMTs, and emergency rescue person-
ᵢ Disaster Response System, which utilizes private heli-
ᵢing medical teams to disaster sites where large numbers
ᵐⁿ burned. Collects burn data from New Jersey hospitals
provides direct professional services in New Jersey
ᵣeferral services nationally. Offers consultation and
the Division of Youth and Family Services and law en-
ᵢn cases involving suspected child abuse or neglect.
ᵉness and prevention programs to schools, civic orga-
ᵃre centers; awards. Maintains speakers' bureau and data
ˉᵃlized education, children's services, and research pro-
ᵧ. **Convention/Meeting:** none.

Burn Victim Foundation--Update, quarterly. Member-
ᵉr. Price: Free. Circulation: 1000. Advertising: not
ᵢshes pamphlets.

ˉᴬ INSTITUTE FOR BURN MEDICINE (Burns) (NIBM)
                                       Phone: (313) 769-9000
                                       Clarabella Jones, Dir.
ᶠ: 8. Budget: $200,000. Nonmembership. Partici-
ᵧ improving the survival rate of and developing the qual-
ᶜtims. Provides consultation for development of special-
ᵢⁱties; prevention programs and materials; education, in-
ˉstics in burn treatment and care. Maintains International
ᵧ over 35,000 citations. Formerly: (1968) American
ᵃtion; (1971) Institute for Burn Medicine. Convention/

and poster; also produces films on burn care and pre-

cassettes. **Computerized Services:** Mailing list.

Publications: *Audiovisual Materials on Burns, Disfigurement, and Related Subjects*, annual. List of audiovisual materials for burn survivors and those involved with professional burn care or prevention. Includes educational and inspirational materials on coping with burns and disfigurement. **Price:** $6, plus $1 shipping. ● *Bibliographic References--Burns in Children*, annual. Bibliography of reading material for the education and inspiration of parents, siblings, and professionals involved with burned children. **Price:** $5. ● *Icarus File*, quarterly. Newsletter for burn survivors and their families and professionals involved in the care and rehabilitation of burn patients. Provides news items on burn prevention, cosmetology for burn survivors, and other topics of interest; includes member news and book reviews. **Price:** Included in membership dues; $4/year for nonmembers; $10 foreign. **Circulation:** 4500. **Advertising:** accepted. ● Also publishes *Guidelines for Burn Volunteers* and bibliographies on burns in children.

Convention/Meeting: annual conference (with exhibits) - 1990 June 5-6, Philadelphia, PA.

★11808★ **AMERICAN ASSOCIATION FOR CANCER EDUCATION (AACE)**
401 Community Health Services Bldg.   Phone: (205) 934-7442
Birmingham, AL 35294   Dr. Samuel Brown, Jr., Sec.
Founded: 1966. **Members:** 850. **Budget:** $80,000. Directors of cancer teaching and training programs sponsored and funded by the National Cancer Institute at medical, osteopathic, nursing, and dental schools in the United States and Puerto Rico and other individuals involved in cancer training aⁿ teaching programs. Aim is to improve cancer teaching and training at ᶦ undergraduate, residency, fellowship, and practicing physician levels by viding organized, supervised teaching and trⁱning programˢ ˣᵈical, ᶦ and ᶜ ʰⁱc schools. ᶜ ᵉʳ instit ᵉᵐʳ ᶦᵗ

★11810★ **AMERICAN CANCER SOCIETY (ACS)**
1599 Clifton Rd.   Phone: (404) 320-3333
Atlanta, GA 30329   William M. Tipping, Exec.V.Pres.
Founded: 1913. **Staff:** 300. **Regional Groups:** 58. **Local Groups:** 3000. Volunteers (2,500,000) supporting education and research in cancer prevention, diagnosis, detection, and treatment. Provides special services to cancer patients. Sponsors Reach to Recovery, CanSurmount (see separate entries), and I Can Cope. **Committees:** Professional Education; Public Education; Research and Clinical Investigation; Service and Rehabilitation; Tobacco and Cancer; Unproven Methods of Cancer Management. **Programs:** Ostomy Rehabilitation. **Absorbed:** (1969) Reach to Recovery Foundation, which is now operated as a program of ACS. **Formerly:** (1944) American Society for the Control of Cancer.

Publications: *American Cancer Society--Annual Report*. **Price:** Free. **Circulation:** 500,000. **Advertising:** not accepted. ● *CA-A Cancer Journal for Clinicians*, bimonthly. Covers cancer treatment, prevention, and diagnosis. **Price:** Free for health professionals. **ISSN:** 0007-9235. **Circulation:** 470,000. **Advertising:** not accepted. **Alternate Formats:** microform. ● *Cancer*, semimonthly. Medical journal covering cancer prevention, research, diagnosis, and treatment. Includes proceedings supplements covering ACS conferences. **Price:** $75/year for individuals; $110/year for institutions. **ISSN:** 0008-543X. **Circulation:** 19,500. **Advertising:** accepted. ● *Cancer Facts and Figures*, annual. Report providing statistical information on the major sites of cancer including incidence, mortality and survival rates, and risk factors; data broken down by sex, age, and race. Also includes information on prevention and ACS programs of research, public and professional education, and rehabilitation. Includes charts and graphs. **Price:** Free. **Circulation:** 500,000. **Advertising:** not accepted. ● *Cancer News*, 3/year. Magazine for a general audience on current progress in cancer diagnosis, treatment, and research; includes personal accounts and news of society activities. **Price:** Free. **ISSN:** 0008-5464. **Circulation:** 160,000. **Advertising:** not accepted. ● *Cancer Nursing News*, quarterly. Newsletter providing information on other publications of interest, schedules of upcoming conferences and seminars, and cancer nursing profiles. ● *World Smoking and Health*, 3/year. Bulletin for health professionals and general readers interested in the problems of tobacco smoking; covers medical, social, economic, and political aspects and problems of smoking worldwide. **Price:** Free. **ISSN:** 0161-7672. **Advertising:** not accepted.

Convention/Meeting: annual - always November, New York City.

The financial strength of an organization is an important factor any time you are considering employment. If you'd like a job with a future, you should pay close attention to finances. The organization's annual report may answer your questions, but remember also that every not-for-profit is required to file a Form 990 or a Form 1065 Partnership tax return (if it is a religious or apostolic association) with the Internal Revenue Service. You can see a copy of an organization's Form 990 or 1065 by asking for it from your district office of the Internal Revenue Service. It takes some time to get it, but in some cases, it could be worth the effort. The Form 990 or 1065 supplies the following information:

- gross sales and receipts
- total assets and liabilities
- net worth
- amount spent for political purposes
- name of accountant
- names and salaries of officers, directors, and trustees
- fees paid for fund raising
- cash, securities, and land owned

Placement officers and reference librarians in public and academic libraries are potential sources of help if you are laboring with a difficult research problem. Remember, they too are not-for-profit, so the price will be right!

The worksheets on the following pages identify places to begin your research. They are very selective in the publications they suggest, but most of the titles listed are widely available in academic and public libraries.

-WORKSHEET-

I. Art Administration

   a. Museums, Art Associations

<u>INFORMATION</u>

<u>WHERE TO FIND IT</u>

Call no.

INFORMATION	Call no.	WHERE TO FIND IT
name, address, telephone number of organizational headquarters; names of officers, size of staff; services	_____	<u>American Art Directory</u>
	_____	<u>The Official Museum Directory</u>
	_____	<u>National Register of Historic Places</u>
	_____	<u>Encyclopedia of Associations</u>
	_____	<u>Subject Collections</u>
biographical information about the officers	_____	<u>Who's Who in American Art</u>
	_____	<u>Art Index</u>
history, description, purpose of the organization	_____	publications of the organizations themselves
	_____	<u>Art Index</u>
finances	_____	publications of the organizations themselves
		U.S. Internal Revenue Service

I.   Art Administration

   a. Museums, Art Associations

<u>INFORMATION</u>   <u>WHERE TO FIND IT</u>

                                          Call no.

potential problems   _____   publications of the
                                                          organizations themselves

                                          _____   newspaper and magazine
                                                          indexes

-WORKSHEET-

I.   Art Administration

   b. Symphony Orchestras

INFORMATION   WHERE TO FIND IT

                               Call no.

name, address, telephone number   _____   Musicians
of organizational headquarters;
names of officers, size of staff;   _____   Musical America:
services   International Directory of
                                                     the Performing Arts

                                     _____   International Who's Who in
                                                     Music and Musicians' Directory

biographical information about   _____   International Who's Who in
the officers   Music and Musicians'
                                                     Directory

                                     _____   Who's Who in American
                                                     Music: Classical

                                     _____   Music Index

history, description, purpose   _____   publications of the
of the organization   organizations themselves

                                     _____   Music Index

I. Art Administration

    b. Symphony Orchestras

INFORMATION   WHERE TO FIND IT

                                     Call no.

finances   _____   publications of the
                                                      organizations themselves

                                                      U.S. Internal Revenue
                                                      Service

potential problems   _____   publications of the
                                                      organizations themselves

                                     _____   newspaper and magazine
                                                      indexes

-WORKSHEET-

I. Art Administration

c. Theater

INFORMATION

WHERE TO FIND IT

Call no.

name, address, telephone number
of organizational headquarters;
names of officers, size of staff;
services

_____ <u>Dramatist's Sourcebook</u>

_____ <u>The Lively Arts Information
Directory</u>

_____ <u>Sourcebook for the Performing Arts</u>

_____ <u>Theatre Directory</u>

_____ <u>Theatre Profiles</u>

biographical information about
the officers

_____ <u>Contemporary Theatre, Film
and Television</u>

history, description, purpose
of the organization

_____ publications of the
organizations themselves

_____ newspaper and magazine indexes

finances

_____ publications of the
organizations themselves

U.S. Internal Revenue
Service

I. Art Administration

c. Theater

INFORMATION   **WHERE TO FIND IT**

Call no.

potential problems   _____   publications of the
                                            organizations themselves

                          _____   newspaper and magazine
                                            indexes

-WORKSHEET-

II. Educational Institutions, Libraries

<u>INFORMATION</u>

<u>WHERE TO FIND IT</u>

Call no.

name, address, telephone number
of organizational headquarters;
names of officers, size of staff;
services

_____   <u>Patterson's American
Education</u>

_____   <u>American Universities and
Colleges</u>

_____   <u>The College Blue Book</u>

_____   <u>The Handbook of Private
Schools</u>

_____   <u>Peterson's Guide to
Independent Secondary
Schools</u>

_____   <u>American Library Directory</u>

_____   <u>Directory of Special
Libraries and Information
Centers</u>

biographical information about
the officers

_____   <u>Directory of American
Scholars</u>

_____   <u>Who's Who in Library and
Information Services</u>

_____   <u>Education Index</u>

_____   <u>Library Literature</u>

II. Educational Institutions, Libraries

INFORMATION	WHERE TO FIND IT
	Call no.
history, description, purpose of the organization	_____ publications of the organizations themselves
	_____ Education Index
	_____ Library Literature
finances	_____ Digest of Education Statistics
	_____ publications of the organizations themselves
	U.S. Internal Revenue Service
potential problems	_____ publications of the organizations themselves
	_____ newspaper and magazine indexes

-WORKSHEET-

III. Health Organizations

<u>INFORMATION</u>   <u>WHERE TO FIND IT</u>

                                               Call no.

name, address, telephone number   _____   <u>Encyclopedia of Medical</u>
of organizational headquarters;   <u>Organizations and Agencies</u>
names of officers, size of staff;
services   _____   <u>Encyclopedia of Associations</u>

                                       _____   <u>Directory of Nursing Homes</u>

                                       _____   <u>American Hospital</u>
                                                      <u>Association Guide to the</u>
                                                      <u>Health Care Field</u>

                                       _____   <u>National Health Directory</u>

                                       _____   <u>Medical and Health</u>
                                                      <u>Information Directory</u>

biographical information about   _____   <u>American Medical Directory:</u>
the officers   <u>Physicians in the United States</u>

                                       _____   <u>Who's Who in American</u>
                                                      <u>Nursing</u>

history, description, purpose   _____   publications of the
of the organization   organizations themselves

                                       _____   <u>Hospital Literature Index</u>

III. Health Organizations

INFORMATION   WHERE TO FIND IT

                               Call no.

finances   _____   publications of the
                                             organizations themselves

                                             U.S. Internal Revenue
                                             Service

                               _____   American Hospital
                                             Association Guide to the
                                             Health Care Field

potential problems   _____   publications of the
                                             organizations themselves

                               _____   Hospital Literature Index

                               _____   newspaper and magazine
                                             indexes

-WORKSHEET-

IV. Religious Organizations

INFORMATION	WHERE TO FIND IT
	Call no.

INFORMATION	Call no.	WHERE TO FIND IT
name, address, telephone number of organizational headquarters; names of officers, size of staff; services	_____	Religion in America: A Directory
	_____	American Jewish Organizations Directory
	_____	Catholic Almanac
	_____	Yearbook of American and Canadian Churches
	_____	Directory of Religious Organizations in the United States
	_____	Encyclopedia of American Religions
	_____	Encyclopedia of Associations
biographical information about the officers	_____	publications of the organizations themselves
	_____	biographical directories for denominations and professional associations

IV. Religious Organizations

INFORMATION	WHERE TO FIND IT

Call no.

history, description, purpose of the organization	_____	publications of the organizations themselves
	_____	Handbook of Denominations in the United States
	_____	The Religious Heritage of America
	_____	Religion Index One: Periodicals

finances	_____	publications of the organizations themselves
		U.S. Internal Revenue Service

potential problems	_____	publications of the organizations themselves
	_____	Religion Index One: Periodicals
	_____	newspaper and magazine indexes

-WORKSHEET-

V. Scientific and Technical Research Centers

Note: Commercial laboratories are included here along with those
sponsored by not-for-profit funds

INFORMATION	WHERE TO FIND IT
	Call no.
name, address, telephone number of organizational headquarters; names of officers, size of staff; services	_____ Research Centers Directory
	_____ Directory of American Research and Technology
	_____ American Council of Independent Laboratories. Directory
	_____ Government Research Directory
	_____ Directory of Federal Laboratory and Technology Resources
biographical information about the officers	_____ American Men and Women of Science
history, description, purpose of the organization	_____ publications of the organizations themselves
	other sources appropriate to the type of research being carried out and the parent organization

V. Scientific and Technical Research Centers

INFORMATION	WHERE TO FIND IT
	Call no.
finances	_____ for corporations, see <u>Business Week's</u> annual "R&D Scoreboard"; for others, see the budget of the sponsoring institution or their own publications
potential problems	_____ Three well known journals in this field discuss problems: <u>R&D Management</u>, <u>Research & Development</u>, and <u>Research Technology Management</u>

-WORKSHEET-

VI. Social Services Organizations

INFORMATION	WHERE TO FIND IT
	Call no.
name, address, telephone number of organizational headquarters; names of officers, size of staff; services	_____ National Directory of Private Social Agencies
	_____ The Public Welfare Directory
	_____ Mental Health Directory
	_____ Social Service Organizations and Agencies Directory
biographical information about the officers	_____ NASW Register of Clinical Social Workers
	_____ publications of the organizations themselves
	_____ Who's Who Among Human Service Professionals
history, description, purpose of the organization	_____ publications of the organizations themselves
	_____ Social Services Organizations

VI. Social Services Organizations

<u>INFORMATION</u>

<u>WHERE TO FIND IT</u>

Call no.

finances

_____   publications of the
organizations themselves

U.S. Internal Revenue
Service

potential problems

_____   publications of the
organizations themselves

_____   <u>Sociological Abstracts</u>

_____   professional journals in
the field discuss problems.
<u>Social Work</u>, issued by the
National Association of
Social Workers is one
example.

8

Information About Government Agencies

Finding the person who can hire you and then selling yourself in an interview with that person is the key to getting a job anywhere. Nowhere is that more true than in getting a job with the government. Most government hiring processes begin with your filling out a long application form and turning it in to a central screening office. If you do that and then sit back waiting to be called for an interview, you may wait forever.

Wise applicants for government jobs begin by looking to themselves to discover their own strengths, skills, and interests. Then they find out what kinds of jobs in government make the best use of what they have to offer. They identify the branches of government hiring people for those jobs and fill out the necessary forms. Their next step is the most crucial. They do their homework about the agency and arrange to have a talk with the person who can hire them for the job they want. When a job does open up, if they seem to be likely candidates, the person they talked with will remember them, have their application forms pulled, and call them in for formal interviews.

Various guidebooks will inform you about the process to follow in looking for government employment. Once you know what you want to do and where you want to do it, you can use this chapter to help you identify the appropriate people to talk to and gain some of the background you'll need to talk with them intelligently about their work.

For each level of government—federal, state, and local—there are similar sources of information: descriptions of the work of various divisions of government in individual states' manuals and in the *United States Government Manual* (Figure 8-1); directories supplying names, addresses, and telephone numbers; biographical sources that give information about leaders' backgrounds; financial data; and current literature such as articles in periodicals and newspapers supplying details about the work and chal-

FIGURE 8-1.   A typical page from *The United States Government Manual*.

DEPARTMENT OF COMMERCE   149

and Federal, State, and local agencies. The Director is the Department's representative to the White House Consumer Affairs Council.

For further information, call 202–377–5001.

Small and Disadvantaged Business Utilization   The Office of Small and Disadvantaged Business Utilization was established under act of Oct. 24, 1978 (15 U.S.C. 631). The Office serves as a focal point in the Department of

Commerce's efforts to set aside procurements for the socio-economic programs. The Office, in conjunction with the Small Business Administration, establishes procurement goals for small and/or disadvantaged businesses and women-owned businesses and also provides an outreach network to encourage and assist those small businesses in becoming Federal contractors.

For further information, call 202–377–3387.

Bureau of the Census

[For the Bureau of the Census statement of organization, see the *Federal Register* of Sept. 16, 1975, 40 FR 42765]

The Bureau of the Census was established as a permanent office by act of March 6, 1902 (32 Stat. 51). The major functions of the Bureau are authorized by the Constitution, which provides that a census of population shall be taken every 10 years, and by laws codified as title 13 of the United States Code. The law also provides that the information collected by the Bureau from individual persons, households, or establishments be kept strictly confidential and be used only for statistical purposes.

The Bureau is a general purpose, statistical agency that collects, tabulates, and publishes a wide variety of statistical data about the people and the economy of the Nation. These data are utilized by the Congress, by the executive branch, and by the public generally in the development and evaluation of economic and social programs.

In addition to its headquarters at Suitland, MD, the Bureau includes a Data Preparation Division at Jeffersonville, IN, a Personal Census Service Branch at Pittsburg, KS, and 12 regional offices.

The principal functions of the Bureau include:

—decennial censuses of population and housing;

—quinquennial censuses of agriculture, State and local governments, manufacturers, mineral industries, distributive trades, construction industries, and transportation;

—current surveys that provide information on many of the subjects covered in the censuses at monthly, quarterly, annual, or other intervals;

—compilation of current statistics on U.S. foreign trade, including data on imports, exports, and shipping;

—special censuses at the request and expense of States and local government units;

—publication of estimates and projections of the population;

—current data on population and housing characteristics; and

—current reports on manufacturing, retail and wholesale trade, services, construction, imports and exports, State and local government finances and employment, and other subjects.

The principal products of the Bureau are its printed reports, computer tapes, and special tabulations. However, it also produces statistical compendia, catalogs, guides, and directories that are useful in locating information on specific subjects. Upon request, the Bureau makes searches of decennial census records and furnishes certificates to individuals for use as evidence of age, relationship, or place of birth. A fee is charged for such searches.

Reprinted from *The United States Government Manual*, 1989/90, by permission of the Office of the Federal Register.

lenges in various areas of government. These sources are available in most libraries of any size. Newspaper indexes and indexes to periodicals and documents in public affairs and the social sciences give access to information about current events in various levels of government.

A huge and very important source of information about the work of the United States government is the government itself. The United States government is the biggest publisher in this country. U. S. federal documents are regularly deposited in large public and academic libraries and are available for the use of all U. S. citizens. Government documents collections are complex in their arrangement and nearly always require the help of librarians in using them, but your extra effort will be well rewarded.

Normally state government documents may be found in large state libraries or state university libraries. The newspaper published in the capital city or in major cities in a state is often the best source for current detailed information about the activities of a state government. For example, if you were interested in going to work on the staff of a candidate for the office of Governor of Georgia, an article like this one from *The Atlanta Constitution* (Figure 8-2) detailing aspects of an emerging campaign would be helpful to you in preparing for interviews.

You can follow the activities of county and local governments in local newspapers. Public libraries are sometimes depositories for the publications of local government, but you often have to go directly to the municipal offices to study these. Annual reports published by agencies on all levels are especially useful, but the surest way to get one is to request a copy directly from the agency.

The worksheets below give specific titles of library sources you can use to find details. Your search may be difficult and involved at times, but if you do your research well, you'll be on your way to a job with the government, and it will be the best possible government job for you.

FIGURE 8-2.   Article from *The Atlanta Constitution*.

Young gears up for statewide race

Gubernatorial bid officially begins today

By A.L. May
Staff writer

After years of speculation about his gubernatorial ambitions and his chances of achieving them, former Mayor Andrew Young will formally announce his candidacy tonight and then jump into a van headed for the back roads of Georgia and an unprecedented political odyssey.

A Young campaign has finally materialized — run by a troika, boasting 11 paid staff members, employing five political consultants based in Washington and San Francisco, and claiming 500 volunteers.

Even the candidate — a sphinx of a politician — has been psyching himself for the effort.

"My campaign folk get upset when I say this, but I don't want a runoff," Mr. Young told a meeting of the Southside Public Officials last week — bold talk for someone trying to be the first black governor of Georgia.

Polls suggest that the former Atlanta mayor and Lt. Gov. Zell Miller share the lead among Democratic voters for their party's nomination, but two respected state legislators — Sen. Roy E. Barnes (D-Mableton) and Rep. Lauren W. McDonald Jr. (D-Commerce) — make the chances remote that one candidate is going to get more than 50 percent in the July 17 primary.

Andrew Young's first campaign tour

- **Tuesday:** Athens, Elberton, Augusta and Waynesboro.
- **Wednesday:** Savannah, Waycross, Thomasville and Albany.
- **Thursday:** Columbus, Warm Springs, Carrollton, Rome, Dalton and Atlanta.
- **Friday:** Fort Valley and Macon.

YOUNG Continued on **D3** ▶

-WORKSHEET-

I.   Government - Federal

<u>INFORMATION</u>

<u>WHERE TO FIND IT</u>

Call no.

name, address, telephone number
of organizational headquarters;
names of officers, size of staff;
services

_____   <u>U.S. Government Manual</u>

_____   <u>Congressional Directory</u>

_____   <u>Congressional Staff Directory</u>

_____   <u>Federal Staff Directory</u>

_____   <u>U.S. Government Policy and
Supporting Positions</u> (The
"Plum Book")

_____   <u>The Prune Book</u>

_____   <u>Federal Executive Directory</u>

_____   <u>Congressional Yellow Book</u>

_____   <u>Taylor's Encyclopedia of Government
Officials: Federal and State</u>

biographical information about
the officers

_____   <u>Congressional Staff
Directory</u>

_____   <u>Almanac of American Politics</u>

_____   <u>Who's Who in American
Politics</u>

_____   <u>Politics in America:
The 101st Congress</u>

I.   Government - Federal

<u>INFORMATION</u>   <u>WHERE TO FIND IT</u>

                                        Call no.

history, description, purpose   _____   <u>U. S. Government Manual</u>
of the organization

                                        _____   Schapsmeier, Edward L.
                                                       <u>Political Parties and</u>
                                                       <u>Civil Action Groups</u>

                                                       career information issued
                                                       by the agency itself

finances   _____   U. S. Office of Management
                                                       and Budget. <u>Budget of the</u>
                                                       <u>United States Government</u>

                                        _____   <u>Statistical Abstract of the</u>
                                                       <u>United States</u>

                                        _____   <u>Moody's Municipal and</u>
                                                       <u>Government Manual</u>

potential problems   _____   <u>Federal Register</u>

                                        _____   <u>National Journal</u>

                                        _____   newspapers, magazines
                                                       and books dealing with
                                                       current affairs

-WORKSHEET-

II. Government - State

INFORMATION

WHERE TO FIND IT

Call no.

name, address, telephone number
of organizational headquarters;
names of officers, size of staff;
services

_____   The Book of the States

_____   National Directory of State
Agencies

_____   State Elective Officials
and the Legislatures
(Supplement 1 to The
Book of the States)

_____   State Administrative
Officials Classified by
Function (Supplement 3
to The Book of the States)

_____   State Legislative Leadership
Committees, and Staff
(Supplement 2 to The Book
of the States)

_____   Taylor's Encyclopedia of Government
Officials: Federal and State

manual of each state

telephone directory for a
state's government

II. Government - State

INFORMATION	WHERE TO FIND IT
	Call no.
biographical information about the officers	_____ Who's Who in American Politics
	_____ Almanac of American Politics
	manual of each state
history, description, purpose of the organization	manual of each state
finances	_____ U. S. Bureau of the Census. State Government Finances
	_____ Moody's Municipal and Government Manual
	manual of each state
potential problems	_____ Public Administration Review
	newspaper articles
	clipping files and reports in the state library

-WORKSHEET-

III. Government - Local

INFORMATION

WHERE TO FIND IT

Call no.

name, address, telephone number
of organizational headquarters;
names of officers, size of staff;
services

_____   Municipal Yearbook

_____   County and City Data Book

biographical information about
the officers

_____   Who's Who in American
Politics

_____   Who's Who in Local
Government Management

newspaper articles

history, description, purpose
of the organization

reports from city county
government on file in their
offices or the local public
library

local newspaper articles

finances

_____   Municipal Yearbook

_____   County and City Data Book

III. Government - Local

INFORMATION	WHERE TO FIND IT
	Call no.
finances (cont.)	_____ U.S. Bureau of the Census. <u>City Government Finances</u>
	_____ <u>Moody's Municipal and Government Manual</u>
	files at government headquarters
potential problems	_____ <u>Municipal Yearbook</u>
	_____ <u>Current Municipal Problems</u>
	_____ <u>Public Management</u>
	_____ <u>National Civic Review</u>
	local newspaper articles
	clipping files at local public library

9
Where Would You Like To Be?

If you think you already have a pretty good idea of what a place would be like, remember that in 1985 the *Places Rated Almanac* rated Pittsburgh the best place to live in the United States. If that was a surprise to you, you'll have to admit cities change, and there can be a lot more to choosing a place to live today than you may have thought. In fact, in 1989 the same publication chose Seattle as the best place to live; while Pittsburgh ranked third. Choosing to take a job in a given location means committing yourself and others, if there are others to consider, to a place and a way of life you may either endure or enjoy for years. If you know the trade-offs ahead of time, you can at least weight them properly in your decision making.

Where can you find information about a location? Before you visit a place, visit your library. Factors important in choosing a place to live are numerous. The history of a place has made it what it is and provides the point of departure for all change. Cost of living will make a difference in whether you would accept a given salary in one place instead of holding out for a higher one elsewhere. Some people are concerned about day care, schools, health care, or care for the elderly. Entertainment, recreational facilities, and cultural life are important too.

The easiest way to do your research in the library is to use any of these publications: *Places Rated Almanac, Cities of Opportunity,* or *Cities of the United States.* All give comprehensive data about a large number of American cities and can make your work relatively effortless. If for some reason these books are not available in your library, or you want greater detail about a specific aspect, use some of the other sources on the worksheet.

For recent, in-depth information about cities, use indexes to periodicals to find articles in magazines. In some libraries, the librarians can point out file folders of information on selected cities (particularly theirs). Ask a librarian if there is anything in the "vertical file" on your city of interest. Another possibility for getting very recent information about a city is the *New York Times'* Sunday travel section feature entitled "What's Doing In...." You can find an article on a particular city by looking in the *New York Times Index* under "Travel and Vacations" and then under the name of the city.

Minority and special interest groups often publish directories. You may want to refer to those to gauge the presence and level of activity of your particular group in the location you are considering.

Once you have travelled to the new city, you can gather more timely and specific information. Details of housing prices, entertainment, restaurants, cultural events, museum hours, etc. will appear in the local paper, free newspapers, and possibly tourist information available in hotels and airport newsstands. Real estate agencies or other sources of information your employer may recommend such as the housing office of a university or a relocation specialist can also give you details about housing situations.

During a visit you can get answers to questions about the less tangible aspects of life in the city such as the level of public civility, how it is there for a particular minority group, or how safe you would be walking through a given neighborhood. If the community is family oriented, and you are single or if the sidewalks roll up at 7:00 p.m., and you like to go out at night, you need to think about the ways these conditions could affect your personal happiness.

Before you decide on a specific place to live in the new location, thoroughly investigate factors like: how long it will take to get to your new job by car (in traffic), on public transportation, or on foot if that's a possibility, and what the relative expenses for transportation will be. Your first year in a new job is no time to be hampered by logistical problems you could have avoided in the first place.

If you are considering a move to a large city, all of the sources on the worksheet will help. To find out about suburbs or small towns, you may have to write chambers of commerce or just go there and ask your own questions on the scene. If you still need more information, use the sources below to get addresses.

If you have a choice about moving, your own research should help make it your best choice. Pittsburgh or Seattle may be the best places to live for many, but they may not be for you.

Addresses:

1. Chambers of commerce: telephone directory for city of interest or the *World Wide Chamber of Commerce Directory*
2. Newspaper: *Gale Directory of Publications*
3. Public school system: *Patterson's American Education*
4. Local government: *The Municipal Yearbook*
5. Locations and chapters of national organizations: Use the *Encyclopedia of Associations* to find the address and telephone number for the headquar-

ters. Call or write for answers to your specific questions or request their published directories.

6. Churches or other not-for-profits or local organizations: Use the *Yellow Pages* of the city's telephone book under "Churches", or "Associations", etc. or see the *Directory of Directories* in your library to find out about the directories of special groups.

-WORKSHEET-

<u>INFORMATION</u>

<u>WHERE TO FIND IT</u>

Call no.

general description of the city
(climate, economy, education, history,
government, population)

article in a general
encyclopedia (see index
under name of city)

_____   <u>Cities of the United States</u>

_____   Editor & Publisher.
<u>Market Guide</u>

_____   <u>Survey of Buying Power Data
Service</u>

library's card catalog:
under subject headings-

"[City]. Description.
Guidebooks."
"[City]. Economic
 Conditions."
"[City]. History."
"[City]. Metropolitan Area.
Description."
"[City]. Metropolitan Area.
Economic Conditions," etc.

chamber of commerce in city
of interest

newspapers in city of
interests

INFORMATION	WHERE TO FIND IT
	Call no.
general description of the city (climate, economy, education, history, government, population, cont.)	_____ New York Times "Travel" section on Sundays - "What's Doing in..." series (find city of interest in the Index to The New York Times under "Travel and Vacations"
	_____ find articles in periodicals by looking in Reader's Guide to Periodical Literature under the name of the city or state
ratings and comparisons of cities by a number of factors (economy, climate, schools, housing, transportation, etc.)	_____ Places Rated Almanac
	_____ Cities of Opportunity
	library's card catalog: under subject headings-
	"Quality of Life-United States-Statistics" "Cities and Towns-United States-Statistics" "Social Indicators-United States"

INFORMATION	WHERE TO FIND IT
	Call no.
ratings and comparisons of cities by a number of factors (economy, climate, schools, housing, transportation, cont.)	_____ find articles in periodicals by looking in Reader's Guide to Periodical Literature under "Cities and Towns" or in Magazine Index under "Cities and Towns-Rating"
climate	_____ World Almanac and Book of Facts "Climate - U.S." in the index
	_____ The Weather Almanac
	_____ Weather of U.S. Cities
cost of living	_____ Cost of Living Index
	_____ Cost of Living News
taxes	for small cities and towns, write to the local chamber of commerce or the finance officer of the city (see Municipal Yearbook)
	for state taxes, see:
	_____ Commerce Clearing House. State Tax Guide
	_____ Prentice Hall, Inc. All States Tax Guide

INFORMATION	WHERE TO FIND IT
	Call no.
crime	_____ U.S. Federal Bureau of Investigation. Uniform Crime Reports for the United States
cultural resources	_____ The Official Museum Directory
	_____ Festivals Sourcebook
	_____ Guide to Fairs and Festivals in the United States
	_____ American Library Directory
	_____ Musical America: International Directory of the Performing Arts
education	_____ Patterson's American Education
	Patterson's Guide to Independent Secondary Schools
	_____ The Handbook of Private Schools
	any of the good guides to American colleges and universities such as: The College Blue Book, Lovejoy's College Guide, Comparative Guide to American Colleges

INFORMATION	WHERE TO FIND IT
	Call no.
health and environmental factors	_____ American Hospital Association Guide to the Health Care Field
	_____ Shakman, Robert. Where You Live May Be Hazardous to Your Health
housing	local newspaper in city of interest
	chambers of commerce
media	_____ Gale Directory of Publications (lists newspapers and other publications in specific cities)
	_____ Broadcasting/Cablecasting Yearbook (gives radio and television stations by city)
government	_____ Municipal Yearbook
	_____ Moody's Municipal and Government Manual
	_____ The Book of States

INFORMATION   <u>WHERE TO FIND IT</u>

                               Call no.

recreation   _____   <u>Wheeler's Recreational Vehicle Resort
                                      and Campground Guide</u>

                      _____   U.S. Dept. of the Interior
                                      <u>The National Parks Index</u>

                      _____   <u>Rand McNally National Park Guide</u>

10
Saving The Best For Last

In finding out about their best potential corporate employers, some people ask:

Question: Is there a list of average starting salaries that various U.S. corporations pay graduates?

Answer: No such list exists. Some placement offices publish starting salary statistics for their graduates by fields each year, but that is as specific as they get. Business schools also publish average starting salaries for their graduates as a group and lists of the companies they went to.

Question: What are salary ranges nationally for the kind of work I do?

Answer: See *The American Almanac of Jobs and Salaries* by John W. Wright. It gives salaries for employees in a wide range of occupations besides business: government, various professions, science and technology, health care, the trades, etc. Or see the *Occupational Outlook Handbook* published by the U.S. Department of Labor's Bureau of Labor Statistics. By the time the handbook comes out, the information is a few years out of date (for example, the 1988/89 edition gives information from 1986), but most libraries of any size will have it. It lists professional and trade associations to which you can write for the latest information on a specific field.

You can also use annual surveys published by trade and professional groups in various magazines. To find a survey, look in the *Guide to Special Issues and Indexes of Periodicals* or *Special Issues Index* under your area of interest (for example, "Accounting" and then under "Salary Surveys").

Salaries for executives are surveyed annually by the Conference Board. Their survey gives benchmarks for executives at various levels in various types of business.

> *Top Executive Compensation.* New York: The Conference Board (annual).
> *Guide to Special Issues and Indexes of Periodicals.* 3d ed. Miriam Uhlan. New York: Special Libraries Association, 1985.
> *Special Issues Index: Specialized Contents of Business, Industrial, and Consumer Journals.* Robert Sicignano and Doris Prichard, comps. Westport, Conn.: Greenwood Press, 1982.

Question: How well does Company X pay its top executives?

Answer: See these surveys:

Business Week's "Executive Compensation Survey" (second issue in May). It gives the top 25 highest paid executives and lists the top executives in over 36 industries.

Forbes' "Who Gets the Most Pay" survey also appears in May and for each CEO gives: compensation, age, years with the company, and business background.

You can also find reports of the compensation for the individual top executives of a corporation in its proxy statements.

Question: Which companies are growing the fastest?

Answer: See the two annual surveys published by *Inc.* magazine:

> "Inc 100—The 100 Fastest Growing Publicly Held Companies in the Country" (May issue)
> "Inc 500—The 500 Fastest Growing Privately Held Companies in the Country" (December issue)
> See also *Business Week's* annual list of the best small businesses (one of the May issues).

Question: Where can I read about the corporate cultures of various companies?

Answer: Two good collections of observations are:

Everybody's Business: A Field Guide to the 400 Leading Companies in America, edited by Milton Moskowitz, Robert Levering, and Michael Katz. Originally published in 1980, this popular book was completely revised and reissued in 1990.

Levering's *The 100 Best Companies to Work for In America,* published in 1987, is another good source for answering this question.

Of course, you can get information about corporate cultures by reading books and articles about companies—particularly corporate histories. Recently a number of articles on corporate cultures in general have appeared, and some of them have dealt with specific companies. Use indexes to periodicals and newspapers to find them under the name of the company.

Question: How is Company X regarded in comparison to other companies?

Answer: Two somewhat dated books rank companies by various criteria. They are: Robert Levering's *The 100 Best Companies to Work for in America* and *Everybody's Business Scoreboard: Corporate America's Winners, Losers, and Also-Rans* edited by Levering among others. Published in 1983, it ranks companies for categories such as "Pounds of Toxic Pollutants Spewed Into the Air Per Year," or "Total Dollars Spent for R&D." Some less objective categories for rankings are: "Biggest Corporate Egos" and "Worst Business Decisions."

Fortune magazine publishes an annual "Survey of Corporate Reputations" in January. Rankings of various kinds appear annually in special issues of several periodicals, and the following two guides can help you find the issues you need. Look in their indexes under the type of business you're interested in.

Guide to Special Issues and Indexes of Periodicals. 3d ed. Miriam Uhlan. New York: Special Libraries Association, 1985.

Special Issues Index: Specialized Contents of Business, Industrial, and Consumer Journals. Robert Sicignano and Doris Prichard, comps.Westport, Conn.: Greenwood Press, 1982.

Question: How does Company X rate in the area of social responsibility?

Answer: A number of organizations monitor this very closely and publish their observations. Some of them are: The Sierra Club, the Audubon Society, and Friends of the Earth. Consumers' magazines, of course, report on the quality and safety of products.

A new book by the Council on Economic Priorities, a nonprofit group, called *Shopping for a Better World*, rates consumer products companies in areas such as advancement of women and minorities, animal testing, community outreach, and protection of the environment. Another book, *Investing With a Social Conscience* by Elizabeth Judd, published in 1990, profiles 200 companies and lists a number of ethical investment funds. The quarterly journal, *Business & Society Review*, publishes a "Company Performance Roundup" in each issue. Organizations such as the Friends' Fiduciary Corporation of the Religious Society of Friends and at least seven mutual funds evaluate corporations as possibilities for ethical investment.

Three good sources of information on the names of these mutual funds and more information on this area are:

> *Financial World*'s May 31, 1988 issue, "Morality Plays," pages 48-49.
> Amy Domini and Peter Kinder's *Ethical Investing* published by Addison-Wesley in 1984.
> Robert W. Casey's article in *The New York Times*, Sunday, January 7, 1990, Section F, p. 14.

11

Where to Look If You Still Can't Find It

If all else fails, try these:

Daniells, Lorna M. *Business Information Sources.* Rev.ed. Berkeley: University of California Press, 1985.This is *the* book for details about sources of business information. For years the author was the head of the Reference Department at the Harvard Business School's Baker Library. Unfortunately, we can't ask her our questions, but you may be sure that no business reference librarian is ever going to be very far from her book. Just ask to see it.

Strauss, Diane W. *Handbook of Business Information.* Englewood, Colorado: Libraries Unlimited, 1988. The most recent comprehensive guide to business literature, Strauss's book was written to be user friendly. It explains basic business concepts and discusses the best sources to use to find information about them.

Directories in Print. Detroit, Mich.: Gale Research Co. (biennial, with supplements). If you are still trying to find directory information, look here. This is the biggest list of directories you'll find, and you'll find it in nearly every library. Look in the subject index for a term describing the field you're interested in, for example, "actuaries," and if there is a directory in that field, you'll find a listing with information that will help you order the directory if you can't get it any other way.

Encyclopedia of Associations. Detroit, Mich.: Gale Research Co. (annual). (For description see page 62.)

National Trade and Professional Associations of the United States. Washington, D. C.: Columbia Books, Inc.(annual). If nobody seems to be collecting information in your field (for example, wholesaling floppy disks), try these directories. They list trade or professional associations working in hundreds of areas—by subject or by key word. You can then call or write them for more information.

Washington Researchers, Ltd. *How to Find Information About Companies.* Washington, D. C.: 1989. If you think you'd like to know about a company's dealings with government on various levels—whether it's reporting to the SEC, answering questions about pollution, or appearing in hearings, use this book to get details. It also gives specific information about requesting the Form 990 from the Internal Revenue Service and other items of interest you can request from the government.

Directory of Online Databases. New York: Cuadra/Elsevier (quarterly). If you want to find a database of any kind, this is the most complete, up-to-date directory of all. It will give you a brief description of a database and tell you how to get access to it. Because new databases are being developed all the time, its currency makes it particularly helpful.

Can't find a biographical sketch of someone? Try *Biography and Genealogy Master Index.* 2d ed. Detroit: Gale Research Co., 1980 (issued with supplements). People known nationally in a field are usually written up in a biographical reference book. The easiest way to look for them is to start with this index. You may have to go to a large library to find the index and the sources it refers you to, but the effort can pay off where others have failed.

If you still can't find anything, write to the organization's headquarters for a biographical sketch.

If you'll settle for just a telephone number and an address for a small business, you may be able to find a telephone book covering the place where the business is. If it's in a small town, that's about the only way you'll get the name and address (short of a computer search).

If the company is in a larger city, you may be able to find its telephone directory in a telephone book collection in a large academic or public library. Or you may find a microfiche set of telephone books called *Phonefiche.*

If you are looking for an institution, and your library doesn't have more specialized directories, try the *National Directory of Address and Telephone Numbers,* New York: Concord Reference Books, Inc. (annual).

For an all around listing of educational institutions, museums, libraries, research institutes, learned societies, etc., *The World of Learning,* London: Europa Publications (annual) may help you. It gives addresses and officers' names.

If you wonder if there is a book in print on a given topic, check the subject volumes of *Books in Print.* New York: R. R. Bowker (annual).

If you wonder if a magazine is being published or where it is indexed, check *Ulrich's International Periodicals Directory.* New York: R. R. Bowker (biennial).

If you have tried everything in this book, and your library can't help you find the things you need, use the *American Library Directory,* New York: R. R. Bowker (annual) to look up details about other libraries. Then talk with your reference librarian about calling another library to see if you can get access to its collections and services.

Finally, if you want a librarian's help with anything in this book, see your own public or academic library's reference librarian. Ask your question on the spot or make an appointment if you'd like a research consultation.

Good luck tomorrow!

Bibliography

ABI/Inform Ondisc. Ann Arbor, Mich.: University Microfilms International.

All States Tax Guide. Englewood Cliffs, N.J.: Prentice Hall.

Almanac of American Politics. Washington, D.C.: National Journal.

American Art Directory. Edited and compiled by Jaques Cattell Press. New York: R.R. Bowker.

American Council of Independent Laboratories. *Directory.* Washington, D.C.

American Hospital Association Guide to the Health Care Field. Chicago.

American Jewish Organizations Directory. New York: H. Frenkel.

American Library Directory. New York: R.R. Bowker.

American Marketing Association. New York Chapter. *Green Book: International Directory of Marketing Research Houses and Services.* New York.

American Medical Directory: Physicians in the United States. Chicago:American Medical Association.

American Men & Women of Science. New York: R.R. Bowker.

American Universities and Colleges. Hawthorne, N.Y.: American Council on Education.

Annual reports. Various corporate reports are available on microfiche from such vendors as Disclosure, and Q-Data.

Art Index. New York: H. W. Wilson.

Best's Insurance Reports: Life-Health. Oldwick, N.J.: A.M. Best Co.

Best's Insurance Reports: Property-Casualty. Oldwick, N.J.: A.M. Best Co.

Biography and Genealogy Master Index. Detroit: Gale Research Co.

Bolles, Richard Nelson. *What Color Is Your Parachute?* Berkeley, Calif.: Ten Speed Press, 1990.

Bond, Robert E. and Christopher E. Bond. *The Source Book of Franchise Opportunities.* Homewood, Ill.: Dow Jones-Irwin, 1989.

The Book of the States. Lexington, Ky.: Council of State Governments.

Books In Print. New York: R.R.Bowker.

Boyer, Rick and David Savageau. *Places Rated Almanac: Your Guide to Finding the Best Places to Live in America.* New York: Prentice Hall, 1989.

Bradford's Directory of Marketing Research Agencies and Management Consultants in the United States and the World. Fairfax, Va.: Bradford's Directory of Marketing Research Agencies.

Broadcasting/Cable Yearbook. Washington, D.C.: Broadcasting Publications.

Burwell, Helen P. comp. and ed. *Directory of Fee Based Information Services*. Houston, Tex.: Burwell Enterprises, 1989.

Business and Society Review. Braintree, Mass.: Management Reports.

Business Index (microfilm). Belmont, Calif.: Information Access Co.

Business Periodicals Index. New York: H.W. Wilson Co.

Business Week. New York: McGraw-Hill.

Cass, James and Max Birnbaum. *Comparative Guide to American Colleges*. New York: Harper & Row.

Catholic Almanac. Huntington, Ind.: Our Sunday Visitor.

CD/Corporate. Cambridge, Mass.: Lotus Development Corporation.

Cities of the United States. Detroit: Gale Research.

City Government Finances. Washington, D.C.: U.S. Government Printing Office.

College Blue Book. New York: Macmillan.

Commerce Clearing House. *State Tax Guide*. Chicago.

Compact Disclosure. Bethesda, Md.: Disclosure Inc.

Computer-Readable Databases. Detroit: Gale Research.

The Conference Board. *Top Executive Compensation*. New York.

Congressional Directory. Washington, D.C.: U.S. Government Printing Office.

Congressional Staff Directory. Mount Vernon, Va.: Staff Directories Ltd.

Congressional Yellow Book. Washington, D.C.: Monitor Pub.Co.

Consultants and Consulting Organizations Directory. Detroit: Gale Research Co.

Contemporary Theatre, Film, and Television. Detroit: Gale Research Co.

Cost of Living Index. Louisville, Ky.: American Chamber of Commerce Researchers Association.

Cost of Living News. Washington, D.C.: The Counselors.

Council on Economic Priorities. *Shopping for a Better World*. New York: Ballantine Books, 1989.

County and City Data Book. Washington, D.C.: U.S. Government Printing Office.

Current Municipal Problems. Deerfield, Ill.: Callaghan & Co.

Daniells, Lorna M. *Business Information Sources*. Rev. ed. Berkeley: University of California Press, 1985.

Data Base Directory. White Plains, N.Y.: Knowledge Industry Publications, Inc.

Datapro Directory of On-Line Services. Delran, N.J.: Datapro Research Corp.

Digest of Education Statistics. Washington, D.C.: U.S. Government Printing Office.

Directories in Print. Detroit: Gale Research Inc.

Directory of American Research and Technology. New York: R.R. Bowker.

Directory of American Savings and Loan Associations. Baltimore: T.K. Sanderson.

Directory of American Scholars. 8th ed. New York: R.R. Bowker, 1982.

Directory of Corporate Affiliations. Wilmette, Ill.: National Register Pub. Co.

Directory of Federal Laboratory and Technology Resources: a Guide to Services Facilities, and Expertise. Springfield, Va.: National Technical Information Service.

Directory of Nursing Homes. Phoenix: Oryx Press.

Directory of Online Databases. New York: Cuadra/Elsevier.

The Directory of Religious Organizations in the United States. 2d ed. Falls Church, Va.: McGrath Pub. Co., 1982.

Directory of Special Libraries and Information Centers. Detroit: Gale Research Co.

Document Retrieval Sources and Services. San Francisco: The Information Store.

Domini, Amy L. *Ethical Investing*. Reading, Mass.: Addison-Wesley, 1986.

Dramatists Sourcebook. New York: Theatre Communications Group.

Dun's Consultant's Directory. Parsippany, N.J.: Dun's Marketing Services.

Dun's Marketing Services. *America's Corporate Families: The Billion Dollar Directory*. Parsippany, N.J.

Dun's Marketing Services. *Million Dollar Directory*. Parsippany, N.J.

Dun's Marketing Services. *Reference Book of Corporate Managements*. Parsippany, N.J.

Editor & Publisher. *Market Guide*. New York.

Education Index. New York: H.W. Wilson.

Emerson's Directory of Leading U.S. Accounting Firms. Redmond, Wash.: Big Eight Review, 1988.

Encyclopedia of American Religions. Detroit: Gale Research Co.

Encyclopedia of Associations. Detroit: Gale Research Co.

Encyclopedia of Information Systems and Services. Detroit: Gale Research Co.

Encyclopedia of Medical Organizations and Agencies. Detroit: Gale Research Co.

Federal Executive Directory. Washington, D.C.: Carroll Pub. Co.

Federal Register. Washington, D.C.: U.S. Government Printing Office.

Festivals Sourcebook; a Reference Guide to Fairs, Festivals and Celebrations. Detroit: Gale Research Co.

Federal Staff Directory. Mt. Vernon, Va.: Staff Directories, Ltd.

Figler, Howard E. *The Complete Job-Search Handbook*. Rev. and expanded ed. New York: Holt, 1988.

Financial World. New York: Financial World Partners.

Forbes. New York.

The Fortune Directory. New York: Fortune Directories.

Franchise Annual. Lewiston, N.Y.: Info Press.

Gale Directory of Publications. Detroit: Gale Research Co.

Government Research Directory. Detroit: Gale Research Co.

Green Book, see American Marketing Association

Guide to Fairs and Festivals in the United States, see Shemanski, Frances.

The Handbook of Private Schools. Boston: Porter Sargent.

Hospital Literature Index. Chicago: American Hospital Association.

Inc. New York, Goldhirsh Pub. Group.

InfoTrac. Foster City, Calif.: Information Access Company.

International Who's Who In Music and Musicians' Directory. Cambridge, Eng.: International Who's Who in Music.

Judd, Elizabeth. *Investing With a Social Conscience*. New York: Pharos Books, 1990.

Kotter, John P. *Power and Influence*. New York: Free Press, 1985.

Levering, Robert. *The 100 Best Companies to Work for in America*. New York: New American Library, 1987.

Library Literature. New York: H.W. Wilson Co.

The Lively Arts Information Directory. Detroit: Gale Research Co., 1985.

Lovejoy's College Guide. New York: Simon and Schuster.

Marlin, John Tepper. *Cities of Opportunity: Finding the Best Place to Work, Live, and Prosper in the 1990's and Beyond*. New York, MasterMedia, 1988.

Mead, Frank S. *Handbook of Denominations in the United States*. New 8th ed. Revised by Samuel S. Hill. Nashville: Abingdon Press, 1985.

Medical and Health Information Directory. Detroit: Gale Research Co.

Medley, H. Anthony. *Sweaty Palms*. Berkeley: Ten Speed Press, 1984.

Mental Health Directory. Washington, D.C.: U.S. Government Printing Office.

Merrill Lynch, Pierce, Fenner, & Smith Inc. *How to Read a Financial Report*. New York.

Moody's Investors Service. *Moody's Manuals*. New York. (Separate volumes have individual titles.)

Moskowitz, Milton, Michael Katz, and Robert Levering, eds. *Everybody's Business Scoreboard*. San Francisco: Harper & Row, 1983.

Moskowitz, Milton, Robert Levering, and Michael Katz, eds. *Everybody's Business*. New York: Doubleday/Currency, 1990.

Municipal Yearbook. Washington, D.C.: International City Management Association.

The Music Index. Warren, Mich.: Harmonic Park Press.

Musical America: International Directory of the Performing Arts. New York: ABC Consumer Magazines.

Musicians. Omaha: American Business Directories, Inc.

National Association of Social Workers. *NASW Register of Clinical Social Workers*. Silver Spring, Md.

National Civic Review. New York: National Municipal League.

National Council of Savings Institutions. *Directory*. Washington, D.C.

National Directory of Addresses and Telephone Numbers. Kirkland, Wash.: General Information, Inc.

National Directory of Private Social Agencies. Queens Village, N.Y.: Croner Publications, Inc.

National Directory of State Agencies. Bethesda, Md.: National Standards Association.

National Health Directory. Rockville, Md.: Aspen Systems Corp.

National Journal. Washington, D.C.

National Newspaper Index. Belmont, Calif.: Information Access Co.

The National Register of Historic Places and the *Annual Listing of Historic Properties* reprints of the *Federal Register*. Washington, D.C.: U.S. Government Printing Office.

National Roster of Realtors. Cedar Rapids, Iowa: Stamats Communications.

National Trade and Professional Associations of the United States. Washington, D.C.: Columbia Books.

The New York Times. New York.

The New York Times Index. New York.

North American Online Directory. New York: R.R. Bowker Co.

Occupational Outlook Handbook. Washington, D.C.: U.S. Bureau of Labor Statistics.

O'Dwyer's Directory of Public Relations Firms. New York: J.R. O'Dwyer Co.

The Official Museum Directory. Wilmette, Ill.: National Register Pub. Co.

Online Database Search Services Directory. Detroit: Gale Research Co.

Patterson's American Education. Mount Prospect, Ill.: Educational Directories.

Peterson's Guide to Independent Secondary Schools. Princeton: Peterson's Guides.

Phonefiche (microfiche). Wooster, Ohio: Bell & Howell Pub. Systems Div.

Politics in America: the 101st [etc.] Congress. Washington, D.C.: Congressional Quarterly Press.

Polk's Bank Directory. North American Edition. Nashville, Tenn.: R.L. Polk & Co.

Predicasts F&S United States Index. Cleveland, Ohio: Predicasts, Inc.

Public Administration Review. Washington, D.C.: American Society for Public Administration.

Public Management. Washington, D.C.: International City Management Association.

The Public Welfare Directory. Washington, D.C.: American Public Welfare Association.

R&D Management. Oxford, Eng.: Basil Blackwell Ltd.

Rand McNally International Bankers Directory. Skokie, Ill.: Rand McNally.

Rand McNally National Park Guide. Old Tappan, N.J.: Simon and Schuster.

Readers' Guide to Periodical Literature. New York: A.W. Wilson.

Religion In America: a Directory. Leiden: E.J. Brill.

Religion Index One: Periodicals. Chicago: American Theological Association.

The Religious Heritage of America, see Schulman, Albert M.

Research & Development. New York: Cahners Pub. Co.

Research Centers Directory. Detroit: Gale Research Co.

Research Technology Management. Lancaster, Pa.: Technomic Pub. Co.

Robert Morris Associates. *Annual Statement Studies*. Philadelphia.

Ruffner, James A. *The Weather Almanac*. Detroit: Gale Research Co., 1987.

Schapsmeier, Edward L. and Frederick H. Schapsmeier. *Political Parties and Civic Action Groups*. Westport, Conn.: Greenwood Press, 1981.

Schulman, Albert M. *The Religious Heritage of America*. San Diego: A.S. Barnes, 1981.

Shakman, Robert A. *Where You Live May Be Hazardous to Your Health: a Health Index to Over 200 American Communities*. New York: Stein and Day, 1979.

Shemanski, Frances. *Guide to Fairs and Festivals in the United States*. Westport, Conn.: Greenwood Press, 1984.

Shopping Center Directory. Chicago: National Research Bureau.

Sicignano, Robert. *Special Issues Index*. Westport, Conn.: Greenwood Press, 1982.

Social Service Organizations. Westport, Conn.: Greenwod Press, 1978.

Social Service Organizations and Agencies Directory. Detroit: Gale Research Co., 1982.

Social Work. Silver Spring, Md.: National Association of Social Workers.

Sociological Abstracts. San Diego.

Sourcebook for the Performing Arts. Compiled by Anthony Slide, Patricia K. Hanson and Stephen L. Hanson. Westport, Conn.: Greenwood Press, 1988.

Special Issues Index, see Sicignano, Robert.

Standard & Poor's Corp. *Industry Surveys*. New York.

Standard & Poor's Corp. *Standard Corporation Descriptions*. New York.

Standard & Poor's Register of Corporations, Directors and Executives. New York: Standard & Poor's Corp.

Standard & Poor's Security Dealers of North America. New York: Standard & Poor's Corp.

Standard Directory of Advertising Agencies. Wilmette, Ill.: National Register Pub. Co.

State Administrative Officials Classified by Function. Lexington, Ky.: Council of State Governments.

State Elective Officials and the Legislatures. Lexington, Ky.: Council of State Governments.

State Government Finances. Washington, D.C.: U.S. Government Printing Office.

State Legislative Leadership, Committees & Staff. Lexington, Ky.: Council of State Governments.

Statistical Abstract of the United States. Washington, D.C.: U.S. Government Printing Office.

Strauss, Diane W. *Handbook of Business Information: a Guide for Librarians, Students, and Researchers.* Englewood, Colo.: Libraries Unlimited, 1988.

Subject Collections. New York: R.R. Bowker.

Survey of Buying Power Data Service. New York: Sales & Marketing Management Magazine.

Taylor's Encyclopedia of Government Officials: Federal and State. Dallas: Political Research Inc.

Theatre Directory. New York: Theatre Communications Group.

Theatre Profiles. New York: Theatre Communications Group.

Thomas Register of American Manufacturers and Thomas Register Catalog File. New York: Thomas Pub. Co.

Trattner, John H. *The Prune Book: the 100 Toughest Management and Policy Making Jobs in Washington.* Lanham, Md.: Madison Books, 1988.

Troy, Leo. *Almanac of Business and Industrial Financial Ratios.* Englewood Cliffs, N.J.: Prentice-Hall.

Uhlan, Miriam. *Guide to Special Issues and Indexes of Periodicals.* 3d ed. New York: Special Libraries Association, 1985.

Ulrich's International Periodicals Directory. New York: R. R. Bowker.

Uniform Crime Reports for the United States. Washington, D.C.: U.S. Government Printing Office.

U.S. Department of the Interior. *The National Parks Index.* Washington, D.C.: U.S. Government Printing Office.

U.S. Government Manual. Washington, Office of the Federal Register.

United States Government Policy and Supporting Positions (The "Plum Book"). Washington, D.C.: U.S. Government Printing Office.

U.S. Office of Management and Budget. *Budget of the United States Government.* Washington, D.C.: U.S. Government Printing Office.

Value Line Investment Survey. New York: Value Line.

The Wall Street Journal Index. Ann Arbor: University Microfilms International.

Ward's Business Directory of U.S. Private and Public Companies. Detroit: Gale Research Inc.

The Washington Researchers. 7th ed. *How to Find Information About Companies.* Washington, D.C.: Washington Researchers Publishing, 1989.

The Washington Researchers. *How to Find Information About Private Companies.* 2d ed. Washington, D.C.: Washington Researchers Publishing, 1988.

Weather of U.S. Cities. Detroit: Gale Research Co.

Wheelers Recreational Vehicle Resort and Campground Guide. Elk Grove Village, Ill.: Print Media Services.

Who Audits America. Menlo Park, Calif.: Data Financial Press.

Who's Who Among Human Services Professionals. Owings Mills, Md.: National Reference Institute.

Who's Who in America. Wilmette, Ill.: Marquis Who's Who.

Who's Who In American Art. New York: R. R. Bowker.

Who's Who In American Music: Classical. New York: R. R. Bowker.

Who's Who in American Nursing. Washington, D.C.: Society of Nursing Professionals.

Who's Who in American Politics. New York: R.R. Bowker.

Who's Who in Finance and Industry. Wilmette, Ill.: Marquis Who's Who.

Who's Who in Library and Information Services. Chicago: American Library Association.

Who's Who in Local Government Management. Washington, D.C.: International City Management Association.

The World Almanac and Book of Facts. New York: World Almanac.

The World of Learning. London: Europa Publications.

Wright, John W. *The American Almanac of Jobs and Salaries*. New York: Avon Books, 1987.

Yearbook of American & Canadian Churches. Nashville, Tenn.: Abingdon Press, 1989.

Index